WHAT YOU WANT IS ON ITS WAY

WHAT YOU WANT IS ON ITS WAY

RECLAIM YOUR JOY, UNLOCK YOUR
FULL POTENTIAL AND LIVE THE LIFE
OF YOUR DREAMS!

DAIVA PLATH

This book is dedicated to anyone who feels that
they are meant for something more and who is longing to
live with joy, passion and purpose.

CONTENTS

INTRODUCTION

For years, I had been living with a longing. A longing inside of me for something bigger. Something more. Something that would make me feel more alive and excited.

Don't get me wrong; I had all the reasons to be happy. On the outside my life was hardly missing anything. I had a great education, a job, good friends. My family was very proud of me. I travelled to beautiful holiday destinations. I often heard from others that I was an optimist and an uplifter.

In many ways my life looked successful. If you'd met me, you probably would've thought that I had it all together.

So what was I missing? What was I longing for?

That was the question I kept asking myself again and again. Deep inside, I think I knew the answer. The longing was in my heart. No one could see it or sense it but me.

Even though I had many things to be grateful for, I knew on the inside that something essential was missing. It was an inner knowing that felt very true to me. I knew somehow that there had to be more to life. Much more. More joy, more passion, more meaning.

And yet at the same time, I was feeling stuck; I had no idea what I could, or perhaps should, do differently.

I never really had time to sit with my longing and embrace it fully. I was too busy. Yet I had a sense that a part of me somehow knew what my longing was all about. I knew somehow that I was NOT truly living MY LIFE.

As the years passed, my discontent grew stronger and stronger, and so did my search for truth and purpose. I was just beginning my forties when it became very clear that my life needed to change. That I could no longer continue to use my energy and time on jobs and tasks that did not bring me joy and fulfillment.

My longing and discontent accelerated my search for answers in the world of personal development. I immersed myself in books, programs and courses. I wanted to find meaning. I wanted to do something bigger and contribute. I wanted to live with purpose.

As my discontent continued to grow, things on the outside seemed to start falling apart. I found myself one summer, for the first time in many years, without a job to wake up to. Here I was, unemployed, without a steady income and with the strongest desire in my heart. A desire to live a life true to me. To find my way.

While I had many reasons to worry about my situation, I somehow trusted that everything was happening for my higher good. That the Universe was rearranging things in my favor so I could finally start moving in the right direction.

And you know what? Just a few weeks later, I attended my first class at the Quantum Success Coaching Academy. I was on my way to become a certified life coach! I cannot even describe the excitement, relief and peace I felt when I joined the academy.

This was also the beginning of my new life. I felt with every fiber of my being that I was now on the right path. The path that was making my soul so happy. Finally I was doing something that I loved and that gave me so much joy!

A whole new world of possibilities opened before me. A world where I can be, do and have whatever I want. A world where I can manifest my dreams and desires with ease and joy, and without struggle!

My longing was transformed into excitement, eagerness and curiosity. I was fully committed to learning and mastering the secrets of manifestation so that I could create an amazing future for myself and inspire others to live their best life filled with joy, purpose and success.

The Quantum Success Coaching Academy has given me a thorough understanding of the Law of Attraction and other Universal Laws that are working in our life all the time. I learnt that knowing the Laws of the Universe and how to apply them is the key to mastering our energy and manifesting all that we want. Only when we are in energetic alignment with our desires and dreams can we become true masterful creators of our lives and reach our goals with ease (and without the daily hustle). This was a total game-changer!

When I started using all that I'd learnt at the academy in my own life, and later in my work with my coaching clients, I was completely blown away by the results! Time and again, I was seeing evidence that changes in our inner world create desired changes in our outer reality.

I cannot even imagine how different my life would have been and how much hustle and effort I could have avoided if I'd had this powerful information earlier. I realized that I so often had been standing in the way of my own happiness without even knowing it.

But here's the truth. I believe there is perfect timing for everything. I'm sure I was introduced to the principles of manifestation at the best time for me, and I have nothing to regret.

I believe the same is true for you, if you're holding this book in your hands. You're about to discover how to become the powerful creator of your own life, because now is the best time for you!

I've written this book to help YOU move towards your dreams and desires in the easiest and most effortless way possible. This book contains everything you need to know about manifestation and creating the life you truly want. It introduces you to the Universal Laws and how to apply them so that you can live with true happiness, joy and fulfillment.

Knowing the Laws of the Universe is like knowing the rules of the game. If you don't know the rules, you will not win. This is exactly the reason that so many are not where they would love to be: they are not an energetic match to what they want to bring into their life.

This book is the shortcut to everything you desire. You're about to learn cutting-edge information and tools that will transform your life and help you create the life you truly want.

To be honest, this is a book I wish someone had given me years ago. It could have made my journey so much easier!

Today, I wake up each day feeling excited about the day ahead. I feel blessed, happy and peaceful doing what I love and can't wait to see what the future has in store for me.

I believe with all my heart that when you have a vision of what you want to be, do and have, you can make this vision your reality. I know there is greatness in each of you and that you can absolutely turn your dreams and desires into reality.

The purpose of this book is to help you find joy, passion and purpose so that you can manifest your dreams, reach your full potential and make the impact you desire to make – without struggle, hustle or doubt.

This book is an invitation to your most amazing future!

CHAPTER 1

LET THE
JOURNEY BEGIN!

It's not by accident that you have come across this book. Would you agree?

In fact, there are no accidents in this Universe, as we are all connected. We are all creators of our life experience, and we are also, at any given moment, co-creating our life in response to the people, things and experiences we encounter.

You are reading this book because you have attracted it into your life. You attracted it because this is what you need right now. Because this is what your soul wants for you right now. Because deep inside, you know there's more to life than getting through the day, and you want more. Because you are ready to learn and grow so you can step into the very best version of yourself: living your best life, filled with passion, joy and meaning!

My heart is filled with excitement for you as I write these words. I know deep inside that the knowledge shared in the pages of this book will open doors for you into your most amazing, exciting and fulfilling future. A future where you are making the impact you desire to make and using your full potential. A future where you wake up every morning with joy and excitement and feel that you're living with purpose.

I know the future I'm talking about here may seem like a distant and unrealistic dream…

But dreams do become reality! If you can dream it, you can have it. If you have a dream in your heart, you also have everything inside of you to make this dream your reality.

You have not come into this world just to go through the motions, day in and day out. You have come here to live your best life, experience joy and live life to the fullest. You have come here to leave your unique imprint – one that only YOU can make.

It's time to start claiming your value and your power to create a life that you love and that brings you all the abundance, joy, love and success you desire!

You Are Exactly Where You Need to Be

The very first step towards your most amazing life is accepting that where you are today is alright.

Yes! Wherever you are today is perfectly fine.

Now allow yourself to pause for a while, take a couple of deep breaths and ask yourself: "How would I feel if I truly believed that where I am today is exactly where I need to be?"

I guess you would feel a little bit of relief, or maybe a lot of relief?

I know it can be hard to accept your situation and make it feel alright if you have things going on that are causing you worry, fear or uncertainty, or if you're feeling disappointment, hurt or even hopelessness.

Maybe you're struggling every day at your job and feel like it's sucking the life out of you, and you're desperately trying to find something new. Maybe you've been laid off and you have no idea how you're going to make ends meet. Maybe you're feeling depressed, even if on the outside you look like you've got it all together. Maybe you're having a hard time getting over a breakup and have lost hope that you can ever find love again.

No matter what your situation, no matter how hard it is – wherever you are today, make it alright with you. Accept your situation as if it is exactly where you need to be. Make peace with it, no matter how painful it is.

Here's the thing: there is power in acceptance. When you make peace with your situation – no matter what it is – you feel relief. You feel your power again. You no longer let the situation take power away from you.

When you accept wherever you are – without resisting it – you feel much better. And when you feel better, you are ready to receive better things! How amazing is that? Nothing is more important than that you feel good, because as you feel, so you attract. Your feelings are powerful!

When you feel good, you are ready to take the next step. You are no longer stuck. You feel balanced and calm and hopeful.

Don't waste your precious time and energy trying to understand why certain things have happened to you. Even if you try really hard to understand, you most likely won't find the answer.

Instead of trying to understand why things happened the way they did, look for the lesson, for the golden nugget. Ask yourself:

- How can this serve me?
- What did I learn from this?
- What do I know now that I didn't know before?
- How can I use this experience to create the future I truly want?
- How can this help me make a difference in others' lives?

There is purpose in everything that happens in our life.

The truth is – and I bet you can agree with me already – these things would never have happened if they were not for your higher good. Sometimes things have to fall apart in our lives so that we can start moving in a new direction or building something new. Something much better!

Things happened the way they did because they needed to happen that way. Because this is part of your life journey. Because it's part of a bigger masterplan of your life. Because a higher power – whether you call that God, the Higher Power, the Universe or something else – is always guiding you towards things that are for your higher good. When you trust the higher power, you are at peace and know that all is well.

The path towards greatness and happiness can be painful at times. That is part of being human. Feel the pain. Embrace it. Fill yourself with compassion. And look forward!

And you know what? If you weren't where you are today, you wouldn't have been drawn to this book. Which means you wouldn't be ready and willing to embark on the exciting journey of creating your most amazing and fulfilling life!

Your past does not define your future. Your past experiences have shaped who you are, but they don't define who you can become.

Every moment is a new beginning. Every moment is an opportunity to start fresh.

Where you are today is perfectly fine. It really is. Even if it might not feel that way right now.

The truth is that you are today exactly where you need to be: you are at the beginning of creating YOUR MOST AMAZING FUTURE!

Yes, you are a CREATOR. A powerful creator! It's time that you claim your power.

Your Divine Design

How can you know that you're able to create a life of joy, success and happiness, a life that fills you with passion, excitement and things you love?

Think for a moment about someone in your life whom you admire because they radiate genuine happiness, success and fulfillment. You feel inspired and energized by them. Yet you might have little or no belief that this level of success, wellbeing and happiness is attainable for you too.

Here's the thing. Whatever you admire in others, deep inside, you want this for yourself! And not only that, you have absolutely everything it takes inside of you to make it happen for you!

The people you are drawn to and who inspire you bring forth in you the same qualities that you admire in them. You feel inspired by them because you have the same potential and greatness in you!

You are not designed to struggle and live without joy. Your divine design is wellbeing, success, abundance, love and happiness.

So how come so many of us end up hustling, feeling stuck, unhappy and unfulfilled? Because no one has taught us that we are worthy and powerful beings who have come here to live our best life and claim our joy, abundance and wellbeing.

On the contrary, what we have learnt from our early childhood and adulthood is that life is hard. That to succeed is hard. That there is not enough money. That there are not enough opportunities. That success belongs only to some special people who have been lucky.

We have been programmed to struggle and doubt ourselves. To compare ourselves to others. To constantly prove our worth. We don't think that we are capable of outstanding accomplishments because we did not learn to believe in ourselves. No wonder we end up struggling and feeling unhappy – what we believe, we create!

The truth is that you are not just an ordinary being. You have not come here to just go through the motions. You are a precious and beautiful soul with unique talents, gifts and skills. You are here to enjoy your life to the fullest and share your gifts with others. Your gifts are also your gifts to the world!

You don't need to earn your right to feel valuable and appreciated. You have no need at all to feel less than others. You ARE worthy and lovable. Already. It's time that you start claiming your value, which has always been inside of you.

The more you own your value and the more you follow your passions and gifts, the more in alignment you are with your purpose.

It's time to stay true to yourself, step into your power and start fully owning your power and your gifts!

Here's the thing. When you start believing that you're worthy of the very best in life, everything in your life will start changing for the better. It all starts with owning your value and loving yourself as you are. The more you do so, the more love and appreciation you'll experience from the world around you. The outer world is a reflection of your inner world.

Stop playing small and start claiming your divine design: success, abundance, love and fulfillment! Know that you are meant to live a great life filled with all you desire.

You are here to live with purpose, to use your potential and make an impact in your own unique way. When you claim your value and gifts, you shine your light brightly and inspire others to do the same!

My Turning Point

Have you ever felt like you're stuck on a hamster wheel that you cannot escape?

Have you ever found yourself drowning under the weight of commitments, obligations and other people's expectations without any time left for yourself and things that light you up?

Have you ever felt like no matter how fast you run and how much effort you make, there's still so much left to be done, and you can't really relax and recharge without feeling guilty and not good enough?

That's exactly how I was feeling for years.

My life was a daily hamster wheel that seemed to have a life of its own. "Did I ever choose it?", I was often wondering. I was always running. I was always doing the right thing. I was always doing what needed to be done. I was a person of commitment, fully committed to my jobs and ready to do the best I could. I was an action taker. Can you perhaps relate?

Nothing wrong with being a person of commitment. In fact, that is a great strength in many ways. I was proud to be a person others could count on, and my sense of commitment has brought me many successes.

But as the years passed, I felt more and more stuck. Stuck in my own life. There was too little excitement. Too little joy or inspiration. Too many shoulds and have-tos. It was as if the hamster wheel was sucking the life out of me.

I was waking up every morning to one more day I needed to get through. I often felt exhausted. There was no aliveness. I was satisfied to be able to cross off the things on my to-do list, but it no longer brought me any joy.

I was longing to be happy and more alive. I was longing to feel more joy. I was longing to wake up with excitement.

Somehow, I knew that I must be standing in my own way. I felt that I was running on a subconscious program with no clue how to change it. It was as if my life was on autopilot.

As time went on, my longing turned into a DESIRE that I could no longer ignore, even if I tried to. A desire for change. A desire to find my way to be happy and fulfilled. A desire to live with passion and purpose and make a difference. I was just beginning my forties.

I did not want to stay committed to the things that had no meaning to me. And to say I "didn't want to" is an understatement; I knew deep inside that I could no longer do those things. I knew I needed to change the direction of my life. It was becoming more and more clear — even if it was somewhat difficult to accept fully — that my job was standing in the way of my happiness.

Luckily, there was a part of me that knew things could be different. That one day I could be really happy. That my situation was not a final destination. This gave me hope.

As my longing to find my happiness grew stronger, I started to increasingly seek truth and relief in the world of personal development. Through the years, I've loved reading inspirational books. That was my shelter after a busy and exhausting day. That was my comfort. The books gave me hope, peace and trust.

I started making more time and space for reading, listening and meditating. I went to bookstores. My home library of books kept growing. I searched for personal development programs and videos on Google and YouTube. I couldn't wait for my workday to end so I could do what made me feel alive, happy and hopeful.

At that time, I didn't know what exactly I would be doing in my future, but I knew with every fiber of my being that in the world of personal development I found something essential for my happiness. I knew I wanted to live with joy, success, abundance and fulfillment, and also to inspire others to do the same and become the best they can be!

Deep inside, I was longing for a change. And here it came…

One summer, I found myself without a job. It was not the change I had planned for or expected – even if a part of me had already admitted by that time that my job was exactly what was standing in the way of my happiness and fulfillment.

I registered for unemployment benefits. That was a totally new situation for me. Not knowing what the future would bring was scary. "How will I move forward from this? Where will my next paycheck come from, and when?" There were many questions running in my head and keeping me worried.

Although I didn't know how things were going to unfold, and although I did feel worried and fearful at times, I also had a deeper knowing that things were going to work out. I knew I was at the beginning of my new amazing life.

I told myself that all was going to be well. I was hopeful. I was open to new experiences. I knew that where I was, was perfectly fine; I was exactly where I needed to be.

That summer, I DECIDED that I am going to follow MY path. That I am going to follow my heart and my passions. No matter what. That I am going to live MY life.

That summer, I DECIDED that I am going to be HAPPY.
I was done with not living my life.

The Quantum Field

Your best life starts in your imagination! What you imagine, you create.

Albert Einstein said, "Imagination is everything. It is the preview of life's coming attractions."

Every time you have a desire or dream, it is activated in the quantum energy field. And because it exists in the quantum field, you can manifest it into your reality!

You are divinely designed to live with joy, happiness, success and fulfillment. You can absolutely manifest all your desires and dreams and live the best life imaginable.

Everything you want is possible because you live in a loving, kind Universe that wants you to have all you desire. A Universe that is filled with infinite possibilities.

The basis of everything in this Universe is energy. This has been proven by quantum physics. Yes, we are physical matter, but we are also energy.

In the quantum field of possibilities, your Future Self, having already manifested your desires and dreams and living your most amazing life, already exists. And because your most amazing life already exists in the quantum field, you have the potential to create all that you desire in your reality.

Your job is to get into alignment with that version of you!

Your thoughts, emotions and beliefs are all energy. At any given moment, you are sending out energy into the Universe based on the thoughts you think and the feelings you have. "Like attracts like" – energy will always attract matching energy.

The better you feel, the higher your energetic frequency. And the higher your energetic frequency, the more you match the frequency of your desires. When your energetic frequency matches the frequency of your desire, manifestation of your desire becomes possible!

Your job is to take care of how you feel and what energetic frequency you're sending out. Every day. Every moment. The higher your frequency, the faster and more easily your desires will come to you.

Isn't that amazing? That is the magic of quantum physics: shift your energy and become an energetic match to what you want!

The Universe is always loving and wants you to have what you want, but you need to master your energy. Only when the energy of your thoughts, emotions and beliefs is in alignment with what you want can you expect to bring those desires into your reality.

All is possible in this Universe because nothing is impossible. Whatever you desire, you can achieve.

Let the journey begin! Expect to get all you want and more. Expect to exceed all your expectations!

Let's Put it into Action

Exercise

Feeling Joy

1. Find a quiet place where you can spend a few minutes peacefully with yourself. Have a pen and a piece of paper close to you.

2. Get comfortable and relaxed, and reflect on the following question:

   • What brings me JOY?

   As you are asking yourself this question, think about everything that lights you up and makes your soul happy.

   It can be things, activities or people. Maybe you love walking in nature as you listen to birds sing and feel a light breeze on your face. Maybe you enjoy doing yoga, or listening to guided meditations. Maybe you can't wait for your next trip so that you can lie on the beach with your feet in the sand. Maybe you love reading romantic novels…

   Think about everything that brings you excitement and makes you feel alive! Allow your answers to come to you. Let your heart speak, and just listen.

3. Write your answers down, one after the other.

4. When you're finished writing, read your answers to yourself, aloud or silently, and notice how you FEEL.

5. Lastly, pick one item from your list that you can easily do in the next few days and schedule time for it in your calendar.

The more you focus on what brings you JOY, the more joy you will create!

CHAPTER 2

NOTHING IS MORE IMPORTANT THAN FEELING GOOD

⸻⊰❖⊱⸻

If you desire to reach your full potential and live your best life, it is crucial to understand and master your emotions. Your emotions have power. Nothing is more important than making sure you feel good!

You may be thinking, "Really? But what does the way I feel have to do with reaching my goals and dreams?" The answer is this: it plays a far bigger role than you might ever imagine!

Your emotions are the key to manifesting your desires and dreams. They will either help you get what you want or they will hold you back.

The journey towards your best life, one filled with success, happiness and wellbeing, must first and foremost be a journey that you enjoy and that feels really good to you. Yes! The better you feel, the more easily you will move forward, and the faster you will reach your desired destination.

"But is it possible to feel good all the time? What if I feel sad, doubtful or bored? What if I can't get excited?"

If you're thinking thoughts like this, I fully get you. Of course you can't feel good all the time. But you can always bring yourself back to feeling good again. Always. You will learn how. You have the power to determine how you feel.

Let's take a closer look at emotions and why your emotions are so important for manifesting your desires and dreams, shall we?

The Law of Attraction

"What you focus on, you get more of"
"Energy flows where attention goes"
"Like attracts like"
"What you focus on expands"

These sound familiar, don't they?

All these sayings refer to the powerful law that is working non-stop in our lives: the Law of Attraction.

The Law of Attraction is always active, whether we like it or not and whether we are aware of it or not. Like the Law of Gravity, it applies 24/7.

We live in an attraction-based Universe where like energy attracts like energy.

And since everything is energy, including your thoughts and feelings, you are constantly sending out energetic vibrations into the world, and these energetic vibrations are attracting back to you energy that is on the same vibration or frequency.

When you're thinking a positive thought, you're sending out a positive vibration into the Universe. And because the Law of Attraction is always working, that positive vibration will attract to you the same high vibrational energy. The same is true when you're thinking a negative thought: the negative thought emits a vibration that will draw back to you the same low vibrational energy.

When you are feeling happy and excited, you attract energy that is on the same high frequency, and the Law of Attraction will give you more things and experiences to make you feel happy and excited. Likewise, when you are feeling down, discouraged or frustrated, you attract low frequency energy, and the Law of Attraction will give you more things and experiences to keep you feeling down and unhappy.

Can you see how it works? Like energy attracts like energy. The energy that you draw to you depends on the energetic frequency of your thoughts and feelings.

What you FEEL, you also ATTRACT. How you feel determines what things and experiences you are attracting into your life.

Once you truly realize and accept this truth, your life will never be the same!

If you want to move towards all that you want with ease and without struggle, you've got to FEEL GOOD. You've got to be the ENERGY that you want to attract! You've got to take responsibility for the way you FEEL.

I love how Joe Vitale explains this: "It's really important that you feel good. Because this feeling good is what goes out as a signal into the Universe and starts to attract more of itself to you. So the more you can feel good, the more you will attract the things that help you feel good and that will keep bringing you up higher and higher."

The better you feel, the more good things and experiences you attract. The better you feel, the more ease and flow you will experience on your way and the more you will enjoy the journey. Only when you feel good can you expect great things!

Your feelings are powerful.

You will never be able to reach your full potential and manifest your desires and dreams if you don't feel good. You've got to learn how to master your emotions so that you feel good as much as possible.

Emotional Guidance Scale

Now that you know that your emotions play a key role in reaching your desires and dreams, let's take a closer look at all emotions.

Here's the Emotional Guidance Scale*:

1. Joy/Knowledge/Empowerment/Freedom/Love/Appreciation
2. Passion
3. Enthusiasm/Eagerness/Happiness
4. Positive Expectation/Belief
5. Optimism
6. Hopefulness
7. Contentment
8. Boredom
9. Pessimism
10. Frustration/Irritation/Impatience
11. Overwhelm
12. Disappointment
13. Doubt
14. Worry
15. Blame
16. Discouragement
17. Anger
18. Revenge
19. Hatred/Rage
20. Jealousy
21. Insecurity/Guilt/Unworthiness
22. Fear/Grief/Depression/Despair/Powerlessness

Source: Abraham Hicks, "Ask and It Is Given"

The Emotional Guidance Scale shows emotions based on their energetic frequency.

At the top of the scale (numbers 1–7), we have emotions with high energetic frequency: Joy, Knowledge, Empowerment, Freedom,

Love, Appreciation, Passion, Enthusiasm, Eagerness, Happiness, Positive Expectation, Belief, Optimism, Hopefulness and Contentment.

In the middle and at the bottom of the scale (numbers 8–22), we have emotions with low energetic frequency: Boredom, Pessimism, Frustration, Irritation, Impatience, Overwhelm, Disappointment, Doubt, Worry, Blame, Discouragement, Anger, Revenge, Hatred, Rage, Jealousy, Insecurity, Guilt, Unworthiness, Fear, Grief, Depression, Despair and Powerlessness.

Each emotion on the scale has a certain energetic frequency or vibration. The lower the number, the higher energetic frequency the emotion has.

For example, Anger has a higher energetic frequency than Revenge; Disappointment has a higher energetic frequency than Doubt and Worry; and Optimism has a higher energetic frequency than Hopefulness.

At the very top of the scale are the emotions with the highest energetic frequency: Joy, Knowledge, Empowerment, Freedom, Love and Appreciation.

As like energy attracts like energy, whatever emotion you're feeling – you are always attracting back to you energy that has the same energetic frequency.

When you feel disappointment, you are drawing back to you energy that has the same frequency. When you feel boredom, you are drawing back to you energy that has the same frequency. When you feel positive expectation, you are drawing back to you energy that has the same frequency.

You see how it works?

Whatever emotion you FEEL, the Law of Attraction will give you more things and experiences to make you feel the same way. You are constantly drawing back to you things and experiences based on the energy that you're sending out.

It is essential that you become AWARE of how you are feeling at any given moment because what you are feeling is also what you're ATTRACTING. It is as simple as that. The energy you are sending out comes back to you.

Your emotions are your inner guidance about what energy, things and experiences you're drawing into your life!

Your Job Is to Feel Good

The Emotional Guidance Scale helps you become aware of what emotion you're feeling and what energy you're attracting back to you.

Let's go ahead right now and ask yourself: WHAT AM I FEELING RIGHT NOW?

Is it contentment? Positive expectation? Boredom? Worry?

Tune into the emotion. Be totally honest with yourself. Let it be okay, regardless of what you're feeling.

If you're feeling any lower energy emotion, do all you can to FEEL BETTER: to move up the emotional scale. Why? Because what you FEEL is what you ATTRACT. The higher frequency emotion you feel, the better things and experiences you will be attracting!

Here's a very important point. No one expects you to go from feeling fear to hopefulness, from hatred to positive expectation, from anger to happiness in one moment.

What you can and must do is move just a little bit higher on the scale every time you're feeling an emotion that doesn't feel good to you. For instance, you can move from feeling revenge to anger, or from feeling anger to discouragement, in a matter of minutes – and this is exactly what you need to do!

Any movement up the Emotional Guidance Scale – even if it is only one number higher on the scale – means emotional relief and also an improvement in terms of the energy you are drawing back to you. The higher energetic frequency emotion you are feeling, the better things and experiences you are attracting.

Taking one little step up the emotional scale is all you need!

Let's keep it simple. Your job is:

1) Become aware of or notice the emotion you're feeling (use the Emotional Guidance Scale to help you).

2) If you don't feel good (your emotion is among numbers 8–22 on the scale), you've got to do all you can to feel better and move up the scale. Every little movement up the scale counts!

I know it's probably totally new for you to start thinking about how you're feeling based on the energetic frequency, yet this is a very important step in creating the life that you want. Your emotions play a crucial role in the manifestation process!

Allow yourself to feel all emotions. Be okay with them, whatever you feel. There are no good or bad emotions; they're all part of your life experience, part of being human. You will feel joy, freedom and positive expectation, and you will also feel doubt, worry, fear and hatred.

We've learnt that feeling blame, anger or revenge is not okay, as these emotions do not make us a good person. The sad truth is that so many of us have not been taught that it's important to allow ourselves to feel whatever we feel. Not to run away from emotions. Not to neglect them. Not to stuff them into our system.

Be okay with feeling jealousy. Be okay with feeling anger. Be okay with feeling guilt. Stay with the emotion. Accepting all your emotions is so important. The more in touch you are with your emotions, the more powerful you are.

No matter what you're feeling, you can always decide to feel better and move up the emotional scale!

To create all that you want in your life, you've got to feel good – and if you don't feel good, your job is to do all you can to FEEL BETTER.

Nothing is more important than that you feel good! How amazing is that?

So How Do I Move Forward?

I still clearly remember that summer when I decided I was done with not living my life. I was so ready to move forward and find my own path – to finally do something that would make me happy, excited and fulfilled!

I did not know yet how my new path would look or what exactly I would be doing. But I had a clear feeling and knowing that I would be doing something I truly love, something that would bring me joy and meaning and at the same time would help and inspire others to live their best lives and be truly happy. This feeling was incredibly fulfilling.

On the one hand, I was hopeful, ready to move forward. But on the other hand, I was doubtful and worried – mostly because I needed to find a job that would support me on my new journey. I needed a steady income that would at least cover my basic needs. How else could pursuing my dream life be possible, if I did not have enough money to pay my bills?

Deep inside, I hated the idea of having to find another job. There was no excitement about this. None at all. I was fearful that a new job would stand in the way of following my new path and finding my happiness. I did not want a job; I simply needed one.

Yet my determination was unshakable. I knew I would find a way! I knew I would do something that makes me happy, energized and passionate. Something that I love doing. No matter what.

As I was immersing myself in personal development books, videos and programs, I came across a leading personal development company based in the US that had helped individuals to achieve greatness and success. I was immediately inspired to connect with this company, and I ended up investing in a few personal coaching sessions with one of their top coaches. His name was Joe.

A few coaching sessions with Joe turned out to be one of the greatest investments I have ever made. For the first time in my life, I experienced the power of coaching and how it felt to be coached by a professional coach. For the first time, I became aware of the importance of FEELING

GOOD and how the Law of Attraction was constantly working in my life. I realized that my EMOTIONS had power and that the Law of Attraction was constantly giving back to me the same energy that I was sending out.

That was an eye-opener! It made me understand that every time I was worried, fearful or doubtful, I was standing in my own way, as I was sending out low frequency energy that was attracting back to me the same low frequency energy. I realized that in order to attract better things and experiences, I needed to feel good!

Joe taught me that every time I had a negative thought, I simply had to stop and dismiss it by saying "Cancel, cancel" before the negative emotion could take hold of me. This is how I would be in control of how I was feeling and the energy I was putting out.

The formula that I learnt from Joe and started applying was: "Feed what you want and starve what you don't want." I was deliberately focusing more and more on all I wanted and giving less thought and energy to what I did not want. That was a game-changer!

Joe also taught me a few techniques to clear negative energy. To manifest what we want, we must know how to release our negative emotions so we feel good as much as possible!

And you know what was also amazing? With Joe, I could be fully myself. I could share my doubts, worries and biggest dreams. I could be vulnerable. I felt so much love, compassion and understanding from him.

Joe made me believe even more deeply that anything was possible if I took action, believed in myself, took care of how I was feeling and kept clearing the limiting beliefs standing in my way.

Joe used to end each session by saying that he was impressed by how well I was doing and that he could not wait to see all the amazing things waiting for me. Can you imagine?! After each session, I felt ready to fly, like the world was my playground. I felt that I could be, do and have anything I wanted!

I can unreservedly say that Joe is an amazing coach who lives his passion. His unconditional love and desire to help me and support me in becoming the best version of myself impacted me in a way I will never forget. Getting to know Joe and being coached by him also affirmed for me that I had a deep desire to do what Joe was doing: to help others be happy and live their best lives.

I felt very much that I was on the right path!

Let's Put it into Action

Exercise

Raising Your Energetic Frequency

Now that you know that the way you FEEL is also the way you ATTRACT, you want to FEEL GOOD as much as possible.

1. Get into the habit of checking in with yourself throughout your day about how you're feeling. The more often you can do this, the better! You can simply pause and ask yourself:

    •   How am I feeling right now?

2. If your answer is that you're feeling good, great! Just continue with your day.

    If your answer is that you don't feel good, or not as good as you would love to feel, ask yourself:

    •   What can I do now that will make me feel better?

3. Whatever it is that can make you feel better, go ahead and do that thing! You know what makes you feel good. Maybe it's listening to your favorite piece of music, or going for a walk, or calling your friend or your mom, or taking a nap, or watching your favorite series on Netflix.

Know that the better you feel throughout your day, the more good things and experiences you will attract, and the more easily you will more forward!

If you want, you are welcome to write a reminder to yourself on a post-it note or a postcard: "Nothing is more important than that I feel good!" Place it somewhere in your home or your office where it will easily remind you to check in with yourself about how you feel during your day.

Nothing is more important than that you feel good!

CHAPTER 3

YOU ARE THE CREATOR OF
YOUR FUTURE

⸱⸱⸱⸱⸱⸱⸱⸱⸱⸱⸱⸱⸱⸱⸱⸱⸱⸱⸱⸱⸱⸱⸱⸱⸱⸱⸱ ⊰⟪⟨✺⟩⟫⊱ ⸱⸱⸱⸱⸱⸱⸱⸱⸱⸱⸱⸱⸱⸱⸱⸱⸱⸱⸱⸱⸱⸱⸱⸱⸱⸱⸱

The journey towards your most amazing life – one that is filled with joy, passion, meaning and success – begins with getting clear about what you want.

Yes! It all begins with CLARITY. The more clear you are about what you want, the faster and more easily you're going to get there!

If I told you that most people never get really clear about what they want, you probably wouldn't believe me – but it's true. They never set aside time to think and reflect upon what they TRULY WANT, what they truly desire for themselves deep in their heart, what would truly bring them joy and excitement and a sense of fulfillment.

No wonder it is so. Most of us have never been taught or shown how important it is to connect to our heart, to go within and ask ourselves what would really make us happy. Instead, we choose to follow goals that we "must" or "should" follow because that's "how it is." Because that's what we're supposed to do. We allow others to define what success and happiness is for us.

Here's the truth. You cannot build your success and happiness based on others' expectations. True success has nothing to do with how others see you. True success is all about how HAPPY you feel about yourself, your life and what you do! Your happiness is the greatest measure of your success. Period.

You and only you can know and decide what is going to make you HAPPY. Not your parents. Not your teachers or classmates. Not your boss or colleagues. Not your friends.

You and only you know what you truly want. Your dreams and desires do not need to make sense to anyone but YOU! You are on your unique journey. You are here to live your best life on your terms!

The Law of Deliberate Creation

"But can I really get what I want?" you may be thinking.

Yes, you can! If you have a desire deep inside, it means that you also have all that you need inside of you to turn it into your reality. Because you are a creator!

The Law of Deliberate Creation is all about owning your power as a creator of your life. This law states that by consciously choosing to focus on WHAT YOU WANT, you can bring it into your life. That which you give thought to, you begin to attract.

You've already learnt about the Law of Attraction and that like attracts like. What you focus on, you attract more of, whether it is wanted or not.

The Law of Deliberate Creation is all about deliberately focusing on what you want in order to create what you want. By focusing intentionally on what you want, you start drawing these things into your life.

You are always creating because your thoughts create your reality. Most people focus on what they don't want, and therefore they end up creating more of the same.

As a deliberate creator, you choose to focus on WHAT YOU WANT in order to bring it into your life. You do not wait and see what the future has in store for you. You do not wait and see what happens. You decide what you want, keep your attention on it and know that you can manifest it into your reality!

There is a huge difference between living by default and letting life happen to you, and living by design as you choose to design your life intentionally, exactly the way you want!

Your job as the deliberate creator of your life is to get crystal clear about what you want and focus on that as much as possible. The more you focus on what you want, and the more positive energy you give daily to all the things you want to be, do or have, the more you will be drawing these things into your life!

Your focus is powerful. You've got to train yourself to focus on what you want.

When you focus on what you want with emotion, you draw these things even more powerfully into your life.

My First Vision Board

As I spent more time reading inspirational books, I got more and more excited about the idea that I am the creator of my future.

Not only was I excited that I can create a future where all my dreams and desires come true, but I was also starting to believe that this is the truth. I was eager to discover and master the secrets of manifestation so that I could create the life I truly wanted and manifest my desires and dreams.

One of the tools I came across for creating one's dream life was the Vision Board. I knew right away that I must have my own Vision Board!

To make one, you arrange images, symbols and quotes or words on a poster board. These items represent all that you want to be, do and have in your future – your ideal future. The more you look at your Vision Board, the more you draw what you want into your life. It is how the Law of Deliberate Creation works: what you focus on, you create!

I found a guide to making Vision Boards on Google and studied it carefully before diving into my Vision Board adventure. I didn't want to miss a step!

First, I bought a poster board and started looking for photos and words that I would love to have on my Vision Board! I went through magazines, brochures and postcards. I looked for pictures on the Internet. I even went to a couple of travel agencies to get their catalogues with exotic travel destinations. I stopped at shopping malls to look at the advertising magazines and see if they had pictures that appealed to me.

My room turned into a creative workshop! I loved the process. Simply loved it. I enjoyed thinking about my dream life and what I truly wanted, about what my future would look like if everything was possible – if it was up to me!

I ended up cutting out tons of pictures representing each area of my dream life. The last step was to arrange the pictures beautifully on the poster board. The perfectionist part of me wanted this to be just right! What helped me a lot in the process was following my heart and my intuition.

Never before had I allowed myself to dream that big, nor had I ever had time to think about what I truly wanted in this way. Never before had I dedicated so much attention and care to creating something that was about me. That was for me. This felt amazing.

And here it was: my first Vision Board with all that I wanted to be, do and have! Exotic holiday destinations with stunning nature. Health and vitality. Financial abundance. Love. A successful career where I live my passions, feel joyful and excited and make a difference. It was my dream life!

I hung my Vision Board on the wall so I could look at it every day, and often. My Vision Board was precious to me; I did not share it with anyone for a long time, except for my fiancé, Stefan, now my husband. He knew he was with a big dreamer! It felt right to keep my dreams to myself in the beginning of my new journey. To hold them close to my heart.

Every time I looked at my Vision Board, I was filled with excitement and joy. The Vision Board reminded me every day of what I truly wanted – and that I could create all this in my life! It reminded me that I was a powerful creator.

What Do You Truly Want?

One of the biggest mistakes most people make when it comes to their future is that they go after what they believe they can accomplish instead of what they truly desire. No wonder they end up feeling exhausted, discouraged or unfulfilled, even if they achieve their goals. You don't want to do that!

As the deliberate creator of your life, you have the power to create your future exactly as you desire. It is crucial that you give yourself time and space to get crystal clear about what you truly desire to be, do and have in each area of your life.

So, how do you get clear about what you TRULY WANT?

Your most amazing future starts in your imagination! How awesome is that? You've got to tune into your heart and allow yourself to dream big.

Your true desires and dreams do not live in your logical mind – they live in your heart. Therefore, it is so important that you turn off your mind, get quiet, relax and tune into your inner guidance. You can only hear your inner guidance when you are calm and peaceful.

Imagine that you are the director of a movie about your most amazing life. It is you who writes the script! It is you who decides everything you want to see on the screen and every detail in the movie! The question you need to be asking yourself is: "What movie about my life I would truly love watching?"

Allow your imagination to run free and dream big. Don't limit yourself. It's not the time to ask yourself if what you want is possible. Be bold and think about how your future would look if it was totally up to you – if everything was possible and you could be, do and have whatever you want!

Paint the picture of your most amazing future in each area of your life:

- Your body and health
- Your career/job
- Your finances

- Your love life/relationship
- Your home
- Your social life
- Your free time

Include everything you desire – the adventures, the successes, the love, the creativity, the fun. Allow yourself to see as many details as you want and enjoy the process! The more realistically you paint the pictures in your mind, the better.

Visualize yourself living your dream life in every area of your life and experiencing joy, health, vitality, success, abundance and more.

As you picture your dream life in your imagination, allow yourself to FEEL the emotions as well. How will you feel once your dreams and desires have become your reality?

Will you feel joy, success, gratitude, love, abundance, excitement? Allow yourself to feel these feelings now. Your feelings are very powerful, and they will help you bring what you want into your life even faster!

As you've learnt already earlier in this book, what you feel is also what you attract. Nothing is more important than that you feel good. The more you are feeling emotions of high energetic frequency, such as joy, appreciation, love or positive expectation, the more you are attracting things and experiences that you want into your life! You've got to be the energy that you want to attract.

Once you've become clear about what you truly want for your future, you've got to keep your focus as much as possible on all that you want to be, do and have! Focus on your future daily and expect to have all that you desire.

Always remember that your focus is very powerful. Where focus goes, energy flows. The more you deliberately put your attention on what you want, the more you draw what you want into your life. You are the deliberate creator of your life!

The more you let your mind become preoccupied with daily worries and problems, the more resistance you will experience on your way. You need to train your mind to focus as much as possible on where you are going, every day. I love how Abraham Hicks describes this: "Never mind what is. Imagine it the way you want it to be so that your vibration is a match to your desire."

If you find it difficult to let your imagination run free and imagine all that you want in your future, here's what you can do instead. Think about all the things you don't want or don't like in your life today. Maybe you hate not having enough money, or not having enough energy, or you're sick and tired of your boss who doesn't appreciate you.

Write the things you don't like about your life down. Then look at each thing that you don't like and ask yourself: "What is it that I DO WANT?" Knowing what you don't want is a perfect place to figure out what you do want!

Let's Put it into Action

Exercise

My Amazing Future

Let's go ahead and get clear about what your most amazing future looks like – the future that brings you joy, success, abundance, love, fulfillment and all you desire! As a deliberate creator, you can design every aspect of your life exactly as you want.

1. Find a quiet place where you can be by yourself in peace and quiet for at least 30 minutes. Have a notebook and a pen.

2. Take a few deep, slow breaths and tune your attention inwards. You can play music in the background if you want to help you relax and calm down.

   - Ask yourself: *If everything was possible, what would I love to be, do and have in my future?*

     As you are thinking about your future, let your imagination run free and dream big… Allow yourself to see and receive images of your dream life in each area of your life.

     Listen to your heart and go with the flow. There are no wrong answers – your inner guidance knows exactly what your true dreams and desires are.

3. Write down what your most amazing future looks like in each area of your life in the present tense, as if you are already living it.

For instance:

"I am living in a dream home surrounded by palm trees and the ocean"
"I feel so happy being in such a loving relationship"
"I love travelling on holidays to exotic destinations"
"I am now a New York Times bestselling author"
"I am feeling so excited and blessed to wake up every morning"
"My yearly income exceeds all my expectations and I am so grateful"

4. As you're writing down things about your future, allow yourself to connect to your emotions. Let yourself feel the joy, appreciation, love, abundance, fulfillment, success…

Read the script about your amazing future as often as you want. The more often you focus on your future, the more you will be drawing what you want into your life!

You are also welcome to add more juicy and delightful details to your script or edit the script as often as you want. You are the author of your life story, and you decide how your future looks. Most importantly, have fun and let this process fill you with ease, joy and excitement!

CHAPTER 4

IT'S NEVER MEANT
TO BE A STRUGGLE

N ow that you know what you truly want and what your most amazing future looks like, you are ready to start taking action towards your desires and dreams!

I know that the gap between where you are today and your Future Self living your best life filled with joy, passion, success and purpose can seem way too big…

Yes, there is a long path to travel from your present reality to your amazing future!

But the good news is that the journey you are embarking on – as the deliberate creator of your life – does not need to be filled with hustle or struggle, nor has it ever been meant to be this way.

The more in alignment you are with your goals, dreams and desires, the faster and more easily you will arrive at your destination!

What you want wants you. Your dreams and desires are waiting for you. The Universe can't wait to deliver to you all that you are longing for! But you need to allow the Universe to give it to you.

Get ready to discover how to stay in alignment with what you want and allow what you want to come to you so you can move towards your future with ease and flow while enjoying the journey.

Let's get going! Your amazing future is waiting for you!

The Law of Allowing

The Law of Allowing is another Universal Law that you need to understand and apply in your life in order to reach your full potential and manifest your desires and dreams.

This is the principle of least action. It is the principle of no resistance.

When you act in accordance with the Law of Allowing, you ALLOW the Universe to deliver what you want. You are open to receiving what you desire. You are not standing in your own way.

When are you open to receiving what you desire? When your thoughts and beliefs are IN ALIGNMENT with what you want and when you feel good.

Whenever you feel good, you are in alignment with your desires and dreams and you're allowing what you want to come to you. Whenever you feel negative emotion or feel bad, you're blocking what you want from coming into your life.

Remember the Emotional Guidance Scale? What you feel, you also attract. You are constantly drawing back to you the same energy as you are sending out, because the Law of Attraction is always working. When you're worried, you're attracting worry. When you're in doubt, you're attracting doubt. When you're joyful, you're attracting joy.

You cannot receive what you desire when you're feeling lower energy emotions such as sadness, disappointment, discouragement or anger because you're drawing back to you the same low energy. When you're feeling lower energy emotions, you are in resistance to what you desire. You are not an energetic match to what you want!

To allow what you desire, you need to be on the same frequency as your desire. You need to feel good. You need to feel emotions that have high energetic frequency: joy, appreciation, love, enthusiasm, positive expectation... When you feel good, you are in energetic alignment with what you want.

The Law of Allowing is all about you feeling good as you move ahead! The better you feel, the higher your energetic frequency, and the more open you are to receiving what you want.

The way you feel is the best indicator of whether or not you're in an allowing state that will let you get what you desire. Nothing is more important than that you feel good!

Any time you're having a thought that doesn't feel good, any time you feel doubt or discouragement or fear, you are not allowing. Any time you are focusing on what you don't like, you are not allowing.

Decide that feeling good is going to be your number one priority. Set an intention to enjoy every step of the way. When you feel good, you're going along with the flow of your desire. Allowing is going with the flow!

Know that when you FEEL GOOD, you are allowing your dreams and desires rather than standing in your own way.

Moving Forward with Ease

Let's take a closer look at how to apply the Law of Allowing to taking action towards what you want.

You need to take lots of action to make your desires become your reality. Action is the key. It's not possible to reach any dream without taking action.

I have a sense that you are already good at taking action since you have a longing deep inside of you to live with joy and purpose, to unlock your potential and make an impact in this world.

Here's the good news for you and all action-takers: From now on, you're only going to take action that feels good to you!

That's great news, isn't it?

Any action that you take from a place of feeling good is aligned action. When you move forward feeling good, you are always in alignment with what you want. That is the Law of Allowing at work!

I love the following analogy by Abraham Hicks about how often we struggle when it comes to trying to achieve our goals and desires instead of going with the flow:

"Imagine putting your canoe, with oars already inside, in a river and floating on the current, and then deliberately turning your canoe upstream and paddling with all of your strength against the flow. And as we see you in your boat, paddling very hard against the current, we ask, 'What do you think about turning your canoe downstream and going with the current... Nothing that you want is upstream."

– Abraham Hicks, "The Astonishing Power of Emotions"

Most people are *paddling upstream* when they try to reach their goals: They are making lots of effort, pushing, forcing. They believe that the path towards what they want must be a struggle.

But if they just allowed themselves to go *down the stream* instead of paddling upstream, they would be moving towards all they want with ease and effortlessness, enjoying the journey.

Paddling upstream means that you are in resistance to what you want. Going with the stream means that you are in alignment with what you want.

Nothing that you want is upstream! You need to let go of the oars and allow the stream to take you where you want to get. How do you let go of the oars and let yourself go with the flow? You do it by choosing to FEEL GOOD!

Decide that from now on, you will only take action from a place of feeling good. Period. No more struggle. No more effort. No more pushing.

"But what if I don't feel good?" you may be thinking.

If you don't feel good, your job is to bring yourself into a place of feeling good before you take action.

Never forget that the energy you're putting out matters. Either you're feeling good and sending out energy that's in alignment with your desire, or you're not feeling good and sending out energy that's in resistance to what you're trying to achieve.

Only when your energy is a match to your desire can you expect to be moving forward with ease! Know that whenever you're not feeling good, it means you're going upstream.

Everything that you want is going to come to you when you allow yourself to go with the flow. What you want is never upstream. You've got to take action from a place of feeling good!

Following Inspiration

One of the keys to allowing you to receive your desires is taking inspired action.

What is inspired action? It is action that you FEEL INSPIRED to take. Follow your inspiration! Nothing is going to help you reach your desires and goals faster and more easily than action that you feel inspired to take.

So often, we make a plan and commit to following it from A to Z. Nothing wrong with that! But we need to also stay open to how life is unfolding and take action based on the signals that the Universe is sending us.

Reaching your biggest goals and desires and living with purpose and joy is never only a linear journey, logically designed by your mind. It's also a journey led by your inner guidance – guidance that is far wiser than your logical mind. This guidance comes from your higher self.

This means you need to both have a plan and simultaneously be open to being flexible and making adjustments as you move ahead.

The more connected and in tune you are with your inner guidance, the more you will understand the ways it is speaking to you and the better you will become at following it.

When you know WHAT it is that you want, your inner guidance will start sending you messages about HOW you can get it, in the best possible and easiest way! When you feel inspiration, this is your inner guidance speaking to you.

When you feel inspired to do something, you can be sure it's a great thing for you to do that will help you on your way to your goal. It is your inner guidance showing you the best way to move forward from where you stand right now – showing you a shortcut, so to speak.

How does inspiration speak to you? It can be an idea that simply feels incredibly good. It can be a sensation. It can be a sudden strong desire to do something. Or it can be a subtle nudge you feel from within.

One thing that is always true when it comes to all the different ways your inner guidance speaks to you is that it makes you feel really good. How amazing is that?

The inspiration you will receive will not necessarily make sense for you; your mind won't necessarily see how the action that your inner guidance is calling you to take can help you to get what you want.

But it does not need to make sense to you! Don't try to understand your inspiration with your logical mind. Your inspiration does not come from your mind. It comes from your soul. Trust it. Your inspiration is your inner guidance. It knows what's right and best for you in every situation. It always guides you towards things that are for your highest and greatest good.

You can choose if you will take the action that you feel inspired to take. It is your choice. Never judge yourself if you don't take inspired action. Be kind and compassionate with yourself. It can take time to learn to follow your inspiration and start trusting it.

Become aware of how your inner guidance is speaking to you, and next time you feel inspired, take a chance on it and take the action! You can rest assured it's going to serve you well.

Remember that your inspiration is guiding you to reach your desires and dreams in the easiest and most effortless way!

When you follow your inspiration, you are in alignment with what you want and you are allowing what you want to come to you.

My Next Step Came via Email!

Have you ever unexpectedly come across something and you immediately knew it was something that was meant for you – you just had that inner knowing that this was it?

This is exactly how I felt when I came across an email inviting me to watch a free video series about becoming a life coach by Christy Whitman, a bestselling author and founder of the Quantum Success Coaching Academy.

The free video series was my first introduction to Christy, and everything she shared and the way she spoke went right into my heart! It was as if she was speaking directly to my soul. There was something so special and unique about this woman.

In the videos, Christy talked about all the amazing benefits of having a career as a life coach and helping others to get unstuck, go after their dreams and live their best life. She talked about the sense of fulfillment, joy and purpose that a coaching career gives, as well as how it can help create financial prosperity and time freedom.

I was simply blown away. Somehow, I knew right away that THIS WAS IT. This was my chance that I could not miss! This was the next step I had been searching and longing for.

The video series was also an invitation to join coach training to become a certified life coach. The one-year-long training was to start the following month.

After I watched Christy's videos, I literally could not think about anything else for the next few days. All my thoughts and emotions were consumed by the idea of studying coaching and becoming a life coach. It felt so right!

But my mind was also asking: "But is the timing right for you?" "First you need to find a job and secure a regular income." "You can't use all your savings and risk getting into debt because you want something; you must be realistic." "Maybe it's better to wait and start coach training next year?" I felt split between my desire to jump on this amazing opportunity and my sense of reality.

And guess what I did?

Just a couple of days after I watched Christy's videos, I submitted my application for the coach training. The following day, I received an email that I'd been accepted into the academy. When I read the email, tears of joy were running down my cheeks. I felt like the happiest person in the world. I felt joy, excitement and also a huge sense of relief. I knew with every cell of my being that this was the right decision. I just knew it. I could not wait for my new journey to begin!

Luckily, the academy offered a monthly payment option, which made it possible for me to join. I would have to cut my expenses significantly to be able to pay for the training, but I was ready for it! I knew I'd made a decision that was going to change my life.

Three weeks later, I attended my first online training class at the Quantum Success Coaching Academy. And my new life began!

Let's Put it into Action

Exercise

Taking Aligned Action

This exercise will help you get into alignment with what you want to achieve so you can move through your day and get things done with ease, feeling good and without hustle.

Instead of jumping directly into your to-do list after waking up in the morning, start your day with INTENTION:

- Every morning, spend a few minutes quietly thinking about what you want and need to accomplish that day.

- As you think about your day and all the things that need to be done, set an INTENTION about how you want the day to go.

  Imagine things going exactly the way you would like them to!

Examples:

o If you have an important work meeting coming up, envision the meeting going very well. See your boss and your colleagues smiling and complimenting you. See yourself feeling happy.

o If your plan is to write a job application, see yourself getting the application done with ease and inspiration. See yourself feeling satisfied and hopeful after you have completed it.

o If you've invited friends over for dinner, see everything going according to plan. See your friends having a great time and enjoying the meal.

You get the idea, right?

Setting an INTENTION is a powerful way to align your energy with what you want before you take any action instead of just moving through your day and seeing what happens.

When you are in alignment with what you want, you allow things to unfold with ease and flow!

Note: Apart from setting an intention for the whole day, you can set an intention for any specific event, task or activity during the day. Try it and see the amazing results for yourself!

CHAPTER 5

FOCUSING ON THE GOOD

————⋯»⋅❖⋅«⋯————

When you've got clear about what you truly want and have started taking action towards your desires and dreams, it is essential that you know how to feel good and keep your energy high on a consistent basis.

As you've already learnt, the energy you're sending out always comes back to you because the Law of Attraction is always working. What you feel is also what you attract. This means that the more happy, excited, positive and enthusiastic you feel, the more things, circumstances and experiences you'll draw into your life that make you feel the same way.

Your journey towards your goals and desires has to be one that you love and enjoy! The better you feel, the more easily you move forward, and the more open you are to receiving what you want!

But how can you keep your energy high when your present reality is far from the desired future, when that future feels like a distant and almost impossible dream?

How can you keep feeling good if unwanted things, challenges and negative experiences cross your path? Let's face it: things will not always go as we want or expect them to.

Keep reading! You're going to discover how you can easily raise your energy and stay in alignment with your desires and dreams, no matter what your current life circumstances are.

The Law of Sufficiency and Abundance

You will never get more by focusing on what you don't have. You need to focus on and appreciate all that you already have in your life.

This is the essence of the Law of Sufficiency and Abundance, which is another Universal Law that you need to understand and master in order to succeed and manifest your dreams.

This law states that you have everything within you right now to create the life that you desire and make your life a living dream.

Just pause and tune into the truth of these words. It means you are exactly where you need to be. You don't need to be different. You are ENOUGH. You are enough as you are, right now. Everything that you need to make your dreams happen is inside of you already.

However, we have been programmed to think and feel the opposite. We have learnt that we are not enough. That we always need to get more, to be more, to gain more in order to prove to others and ourselves that we are ENOUGH.

Feeling that we are not enough is one of the biggest wounds – a wound that has been living through generations and is still active in most people.

Not enough money. Not enough time. Not enough qualifications. Not enough success. You name it! No matter how much we try, we feel that it is still not enough… We can live our whole life chasing more and still end up feeling that we are not enough.

We have been raised to look at what is missing and what is not working. To compare ourselves to others. To compete. To long for what others have.

We have been programed into a mindset of scarcity and lack. Lack always feels bad. Lack makes us feel worried, stressed and fearful. Here's the thing: whenever we're coming from a place of thinking that what we have is not enough, or that we are not enough, that is what we attract into our life.

We have been born into an abundant Universe, but we have been trained to see things from a perspective of lack. Nature does not know lack, does it? It knows only abundance. Can you count the leaves of the trees? The flowers in the meadow? The rain drops? The waves in the ocean?

There is more than enough. Supply is unlimited. The Universe is abundant.

Abundance always feels good. When you feel good, you attract more good things. It's time to shift your mindset from lack to abundance and to connect to the truth of who you are. If you are here, you are ENOUGH. Already. It's time to believe that you live in an abundant Universe and that you deserve to have what you want.

The more you focus on abundance, the more things, experiences and opportunities the Universe will send you to show that you are abundant. Your focus is powerful!

The Power of Gratitude

One of the easiest ways to shift your focus from lack to abundance is by feeling grateful.

Remember the Emotional Guidance Scale? Appreciation is at the very top; it's the emotion with the highest energetic frequency. The more grateful you feel, the more things, circumstances and experiences you will draw into your life that are at the same high energetic frequency.

You will never be able to create the life of your dreams if you keep focusing on lack and what is missing. What you focus on, you attract. This is exactly why so many people struggle to manifest their dreams and desires and to create success: they keep focusing on what's missing and what they don't have instead of focusing on what they have.

Everything is energy, and lack is a low frequency energy. When you are focused on what you don't have, you're sending out low energy, which in turn draws back to you things and experiences at the same low frequency. Your attempts to move towards your goals and desires feel like a struggle and hustle. When you are in lack, you can't receive better things. You are not an energetic match to what you want.

In order to receive more good things, you need to be tuned into high energetic frequency! The energy of GRATITUDE is powerful. It's magnetic. When you start feeling grateful on a daily basis, you'll start drawing good things and experiences to yourself like a magnet. You'll attract more things into your life to be grateful for and start seeing positive shifts in your reality! How amazing is that?

The key to more is being GRATEFUL for what you have. Gratitude will help you transcend any negativity you might be experiencing in your life and raise your energetic frequency.

I love what Oprah said on this; her words are so true and powerful: "If you look at what you have in life, you'll always have more. If you look at what you don't have in life, you'll never have enough."

Usually we feel grateful when something good happens: when we get something we want, when we've achieved our desire, when we've received good news. However, when we feel stuck or when things are not going our way, we don't feel there is much to be grateful for. We think, "Bring me something to be grateful for, and then I'll be grateful."

Don't wait for something to happen so you have a reason to be grateful! Good things cannot reach you when you're sending out the energy of lack. Start deliberately looking for reasons in your life to be grateful for NOW. When you start looking, you will absolutely find them!

Gratitude is a powerful choice that you have to make as the deliberate creator of your life! The more grateful you feel every day, the more opportunities and magic you will start drawing into your life.

And you know what's truly amazing? Nothing in your outer reality needs to shift so you can open yourself to more abundance and flow; what needs to shift is YOU and your FOCUS. Instead of focusing on what's missing, you've got to start focusing on all that is good and be grateful!

All Is Well in My World!

My studies to become a life coach exceeded all my expectations. Beyond any doubt, this was the most exciting and intensive training I'd ever had, filled with new discoveries, new insights, personal growth and new friends from all over the world. I loved it all. I knew I was in the right place. I felt totally at home.

For the first time in my life, I was so excited and proud to tell others what I was doing. I was studying to become a life coach, which was my greatest passion! I felt proud when I said it. I felt joy. Deep in my soul, it felt so right.

I looked forward to every class with excitement. I was open, curious and devoted. I went all-in! I completed every assignment with care and dedication. I was eager to become the best coach I could be!

I was committed to something I was totally passionate about. Something I loved. I was fully enjoying what I was doing. Can you imagine?

This time was also a time for my inner growth. One of the key shifts I experienced internally was my daily focus. I was retraining my mind to look for the good. Every day. If the older me looked for a reason to feel happy, the new me was finding the reasons to be happy – every single day!

Instead of waiting to see what the day had in store for me, I was now:

- *constantly looking for things to appreciate and be grateful for;*
- *counting my successes and celebrating them (I was even keeping a success journal, where I was writing down my daily successes);*

     ○   *keeping my focus on my vision and all the amazing things waiting for me in the future.*

As I intentionally focused on the positives, my energetic frequency was getting higher and I was feeling better on a consistent basis. That was great! If something happened during the day to put me in a bad mood or make me feel less good, I no longer let it affect me in the same way as before. I knew exactly what to do to bring myself into a state of feeling good again. Now I had so many tools I could use to help me feel good!

I also became very much in tune with how I was feeling. Feeling good became my first priority. I knew in my mind and in my heart that nothing was more important than feeling good because my feeling state was directly affecting what things and experiences I was drawing into my life.

I fully committed not only to becoming a great coach, but also to enjoying the journey! I knew that in order to manifest anything I wanted, it was essential that I was happy about all that I already had. Yes, I knew deep inside that the only right way for me to move forward and manifest my dreams and desires was feeling good – in the now. No hustle and pushing!

And you know what!? I did feel that the Universe was on my side. Not only was I fully enjoying my new journey to becoming a coach, but soon after I started my coaching studies, Stefan and I said YES to each other at the Little White Chapel in Las Vegas! That was my dream come true. We could never have wished for a better or more exciting and adventurous wedding!

Looking for Positive Aspects

Another easy and powerful way to shift your focus and energy from lack to abundance is choosing to focus on the positive aspects of any situation.

In the same way that gratitude helps you transform negativity and raises your energetic frequency, focusing on positive aspects will help you stay feeling good no matter what.

Let me ask you: Where in your life do you feel bad today? Where do you feel lack?

Maybe you struggle with money? Maybe you feel unhappy in your relationship? Maybe your current job is sucking the life out of you? Be totally honest with yourself.

No matter what your situation, allow yourself to fully feel and embrace whatever emotions the situation brings up in you. Fill yourself with love and compassion. Whatever you are feeling, let it be okay. Once you feel at peace with the situation, start looking for positive aspects of the situation.

You can simply take a piece of paper and start writing down all the good things or positive aspects that you can think of. Let's face it: there is no situation that is only bad. There will always be something positive about it, and you must train yourself to find the positive.

Let's say you're unhappy about your job. You work long hours. Your pay is too small. You do not feel appreciated. You often feel like there's nothing to be happy about in your job.

Now identify all the positive aspects that you can about your job! Maybe you like the fact that you get to work at home three days a week, which gives you time freedom. Maybe you love some task at your job that you always look forward to doing. Maybe your current job will be the perfect thing to add to your CV when you decide to move on. Maybe you enjoy having lunch with your colleagues.

Write down all the positive aspects of your job that you can and then decide to focus on these positive aspects every time you go to work.

When you focus on the good, you feel good. When you focus on the negative and what's missing, you feel bad. Whatever you focus on, you get more of. Like attracts like!

If you don't want to create more negativity and attract more things and experiences that make you feel down, you've got to change your focus! When you change your focus to the positive aspects of the situation, you change your feeling state immediately to a higher energetic frequency. As you feel better, you will attract better and you'll bring yourself back into the allowing place for all good things to come into your life.

When you train yourself to look for the positive aspects – no matter what your situation – you'll soon notice a shift in your situation as well! Why? Because you will bring a new energy to the same situation. Always remember that whatever energy you are sending out, you are also attracting back to you!

When you can find satisfaction with your current situation – while at the same time being excited about all the wonderful things awaiting you in the future – you are ready and open to manifest all you want!

You have a choice in every moment. In any given situation, you can keep focusing on all the negative things and feel disempowered and stuck, or you can deliberately choose to look for positive aspects and feel hopeful and uplifted. The choice is yours!

Looking for positive aspects in every situation helps you stay in a place of feeling good. And when you feel good, you are open to receiving more good, and you move towards your dreams and desires with ease!

Let's Put it into Action

Exercise

Gratitude Journal

1. Choose a nice notebook or a journal. You can name it: *My Gratitude Journal.*

2. Every day, spend a few minutes quietly with yourself thinking about things in your life that you're grateful for.

   They can be small or big things. Find at least 5 things and write them down in your Gratitude Journal.

3. As you're writing, try to tune into the feeling of gratitude. Notice how you feel in your body and allow yourself to stay in the feeling of gratitude for a while.

Manifesting TIP: You can even write things in your Gratitude Journal that you want to manifest in your future. This is a great way to speed up the manifestation!

Let's say you want a new job with a better salary. You can write, for instance:
"I am so grateful for my new job that I love and that is allowing me to go on my dream vacations."

You can do this exercise early in the morning, late in the evening or during the day. Find the time that suits you best.

Keep your Gratitude Journal for at least 30 days. This will help you retrain your mind to focus on abundance and raise your energetic frequency. The better you feel, the more good things you'll attract! The more abundant you feel, the more abundance you will create!

CHAPTER 6

QUESTION YOUR BELIEFS

⊷·❖·⊶

If the Universe is loving and is always supporting you, then your journey towards your most amazing and fulfilling future doesn't have to be hard at all. Right?

So how come so many of us never reach our desires and continue to live without joy or success, feeling unfulfilled? How come so many of us set off on a journey towards our dreams, filled with excitement and determination, but lose momentum on the way and get stuck?

Why is it that some people seem to reach their goals with ease and without struggle, while others – no matter how hard they try – never truly succeed and keep living the same story?

Is the Universe more favorable to some and less favorable to others? Is the Universe more kind and generous to some of us?

Here's the truth. The Universe is always loving and kind. It is always supporting each and every one of us. But it cannot give you what you do not BELIEVE you can have.

The Universe will always mirror back to you what you THINK and BELIEVE inside of you. Another way of saying it is that your inner world creates your outer reality.

In order to ensure that you reach your desired destination and manifest your dreams, it is essential that you know and question the beliefs inside of you. Only when your beliefs are in alignment with what you want to be, do and have can you expect to achieve your goals and experience success, joy and fulfillment.

Let's dive into the world of beliefs, shall we? You're going to discover how limiting beliefs may be sabotaging your progress and success from behind the scenes and how you can replace them with new, empowering beliefs that will help you achieve whatever you want.

Your Beliefs Create Your Reality

What is a belief? A belief is just a thought we think over and over again – until we believe it. When we believe a thought, we don't question it at all. It has become our truth.

Most beliefs are formed when we're growing up. We take beliefs from our parents, school, friends, social media. We automatically absorb the thoughts of those around us as our own, and they become our truth.

Our beliefs get stored in our subconscious mind, where they operate as an automatic program. We are usually not aware of them.

But here's what is essential to understand: Our beliefs create our life experience. Our life experience will always reflect back to us what we believe deep inside.

When it comes to reaching your goals and desires and creating the success and happiness you are longing for, it is crucial to have beliefs that support you and are aligned with where you're going. If your beliefs are holding you back, the journey towards success can be an uphill battle; you'll find yourself struggling and wonder why things aren't working out for you. You may even conclude that some people are simply luckier, or smarter, or more talented than you.

This is exactly why so many people never reach their desired destination: their internal beliefs are stopping them.

Let's take a closer look at some of your beliefs, shall we?

Think about one of the past successes in your own life. It can be big or small. Something you remember with satisfaction. Something you are proud to share with others and that fills you with joy and makes you feel really good.

As you're thinking about your success, ask yourself: "What did I need to believe about myself in order to achieve this?" The answers that will come to you may be:

- "I can have what I want."
- "I am a winner."
- "I am capable of achieving what I want."
- "Support comes to me whenever I need it."
- "I am lucky."
- "Things come to me with ease."

All such thoughts are the beliefs that have helped you to achieve your success. They are positive and empowering. These thoughts show that you already have inside you beliefs that can help you to create anything you want! If you've achieved success before, you can surely create new success!

Now think about a past event in your life where you considered yourself a "failure" or where things did not go as planned. It could be that you don't even want to remember it because it causes you to feel awkward, sad or discouraged.

As you think about one of your "failures", ask yourself: "What did I need to believe about myself in order to create this?" The answers that will come to you may be:

- "I am not really good at this."
- "I don't really have what it takes."
- "Others are much better than me."
- "It's not for me."
- "Life is not fair."

- "I can try, but the chances of winning are small."

All such thoughts are your beliefs that did not allow you to win! Can you see that? These thoughts were holding you back from succeeding! These are internal beliefs that are standing in your way.

We create our reality from our beliefs. That's why it is crucial that we give ourselves time and effort to understand what our beliefs are.

If you dream of having something but at the same time believe deep in your subconscious mind that you cannot have what you want, you will never have it. Your limiting beliefs will end up interfering with the process of getting what you want.

So, the question you need to ask yourself first and foremost is: "Are my beliefs aligned with what I want to be, do and have?"

I find the famous quote by Henry Ford so powerful: "Whether you think you can or you think you can't, you are right." Whatever you think, you will manifest in your reality!

If you truly believe you can reach your dreams and desires and you keep taking action, you will get there!

Letting Go of Limiting Beliefs

If you have a sense that quite a few of your beliefs are stopping you from moving towards the life of your dreams, please don't worry! We all have limiting beliefs deep inside of us that in one way or another are holding us back from moving confidently towards our goals.

On my own transformational journey, I have cleared a bunch of limiting beliefs that were standing in my way, and the process of letting go of limiting beliefs still continues!

You see, every time you want to move to another level in your career and life, you must ensure that your beliefs are supporting you. Letting go of the limiting beliefs is an important part of the process.

The really good news about beliefs is that you can CHANGE them! We have the power to change our beliefs. Yes, you can deliberately decide to let go of the limiting belief and replace it with a new and empowering belief.

When we change our beliefs, our reality will also change. We are constantly attracting and creating our life experience based on what we believe.

As a life coach, it is an incredible joy for me to see time after time how just changing ONE belief can create positive changes in the client's life. In fact, it can be mind-blowing.

Some of the common limiting beliefs people have are thoughts such as:

- But I don't have enough time.
- But I don't have enough money.
- But I am too old.
- Money doesn't grow on trees.
- But what will they think?
- Who am I to want all these things?
- You cannot have both.
- Good things never last.
- To succeed, I need to work hard and struggle.

Can you perhaps recognize some of these limiting beliefs in yourself?

If you don't CHANGE the limiting beliefs inside of you, they will keep sabotaging your progress towards your goals and stand in the way of your success.

The very first step to changing your limiting beliefs is awareness. Awareness is the key. You cannot change what you are not aware of. The tricky part about our beliefs is that we are usually not conscious of what we believe. We need to dig deeper to find them!

Once you're aware of a limiting belief inside of you, you can decide to let go of it and replace it with a new, empowering belief – a belief that is going to support you towards your success and happiness! How amazing is that?

Here are examples of powerful beliefs that you can implant into your subconscious to replace the beliefs that are holding you back:

- Things are always working out for me.
- I have value.
- I am deserving of success.
- I have what it takes.
- I do not need anyone's permission to succeed.
- I am the creator of my future.
- I am capable of great things.
- I can do whatever I set my mind to.
- The Universe is always on my side.

There are many tools and techniques you can use to help you release your limiting beliefs. Yet the most effective way to change your beliefs is working with a personal life coach. Even the most successful people on the planet use coaches! That is exactly why they have managed to build their success and continue experiencing even more success.

A journey to your success is a journey of personal transformation and expansion. Uncovering the limiting beliefs inside of you and replacing them with supporting and empowering beliefs is a very important part of this transformation.

If you do not have the opportunity to hire a coach, you can seek information in books, articles, online courses and YouTube videos. There are many resources that are easily available to help you enhance your understanding about the beliefs and how they shape your reality.

Always remember that no matter how things have been for you up to this moment, you can always make a new start. Each moment is a new beginning!

It is you who chooses what you want to believe. You and no one else in this very moment can decide that you'll no longer believe a thought that does not serve you and will start believing a new thought that will uplift and empower you and make you unstoppable on the way to your amazing future!

Change your beliefs, change your life!

I Am Enough

You've most likely experienced those moments when someone said something to you, or you heard something, and it was so profound that it stayed with you for the rest of your life.

I had one such moment one day. I was at one of my coaching classes. The teacher was asking for volunteers that she could coach in order to demonstrate how to use different coaching processes and techniques when working with clients.

And here I was, being coached by my teacher as the other students in the class listened. I remember I was filled with excitement and also a little nervousness.

I talked about how much I wanted to become a coach and how excited and passionate I felt about inspiring people to live their best lives. I also shared my biggest worry at that time: my financial situation. In order to pursue my dream as a coach, I needed to find a job that could support me financially while I was studying coaching and while I was building my own coaching business.

As the teacher coached me, I felt even more connected to my vision. I felt my worries being released, and I felt so deeply in tune with my passion to become a coach. I felt so confident that I would of course find a way to make my dream happen. And then the teacher told me something that I will never forget:

"Who you are, Daiva, is ENOUGH... It's not always about the DOING. Who you are – just by your BEINGNESS – is enough."

I remember her words went right into my heart. I was deeply touched. It was as if something deep inside of me shifted.

It was as if my soul recognized the truth: "I AM ENOUGH."

It was as if I allowed this truth to sink deep into my body and soul.

My teacher made me connect to the value inside of me, the value that is not dependent on how much I do, or what I achieve.

She helped me feel the value that is already in me. That has always been in me. That is in every single person. That is in YOU.

I do not need to do anything to prove my value. I do not need anyone's permission to feel valuable. I do not need anyone's approval or validation.

I HAVE value.

I AM enough.

I AM deserving, just because I'm here.

It's not about doing. It's about BEING.

I still have to remind myself of this truth sometimes: I am ENOUGH just the way I am.

I am ENOUGH.

I am ENOUGH, which also means that I have everything inside of me to create all that I want!

Let's Put it into Action

Exercise

Replacing Limiting Beliefs with Positive Beliefs

This exercise will help you uncover the limiting beliefs that may be holding you back from moving towards your goals and desires. Once you know your limiting beliefs, you'll be able to replace them with positive and empowering beliefs.

1. Think about the goal you want to achieve. It can be big or small.

   As you're reflecting on your goal, notice the inner dialogue in your mind and pay attention to any thoughts telling you WHY YOU CANNOT ACHIEVE your goal, or WHY IT IS almost IMPOSSIBLE to achieve it.

   For instance, you might notice such thoughts as:

   o I don't have time.
   o It will cost too much money.
   o Who am I to think I can do it?
   o I never follow through on my goals.

   Write all these thoughts down. These thoughts are your *limiting beliefs* that are holding you back.

2. Look at each thought that you've written down and then find and write down an opposite thought that is positive.

For instance:

o I don't have time >> *I always find time for things that matter.*
o It will cost too much money >> *I attract money easily.*
o Who am I to think I can do it? >> *I am worthy and deserving of success.*
o I never follow through on my goals >> *I can make it happen.*

3. Write down your new positive beliefs on a postcard or a piece of paper so that you can look at them as often as you can. In this way, you will be retraining your subconscious mind. The more you see and tell yourself the new belief, the more you'll start believing it and acting in accordance with the new belief.

CHAPTER 7

YOUR SETBACK IS ALSO YOUR OPPORTUNITY

Now that you've come so far in the book and learnt so much to help you create what you want, you most likely keep thinking: "But what if things don't go my way? What if unwanted things happen? What if big problems arise?"

I get you! You're totally right. There will absolutely be problems, challenges and setbacks along the way. There will be doubts and disappointments. There will be times when you might even want to give up on the journey and go back to "normal" life.

Challenges and problems are inevitable; they're part of our life experience. They also make us stronger, wiser and more resilient. You would not be the person you are today if you hadn't overcome some challenges in the past.

The good news is that you have the power inside of you to deal with the challenges in a way that keeps you strong, confident and empowered!

There is no problem without solution. There is no doubt without clarity. There is no darkness without light. It is YOU who chooses where you're going to put your focus.

Get ready to discover how to master your focus under any conditions, and how your focus will help you move forward and manifest your dreams and desires despite the challenges that confront you along the way.

Are you excited? I bet you are!

The Law of Polarity

The Law of Polarity is one of the seven Universal Laws that you need to understand and apply to create the life that you want.

This law states that there are two poles, or two opposites, of everything in existence. Polarity exists within everything we can possibly experience in the physical universe:

Darkness and light
Sadness and joy
Pain and pleasure
Poverty and wealth
Cold and warmth
War and peace

All of these are examples of polarity. Our Universe is literally made up of opposite forces.

This means every subject is actually two subjects. There is the thing itself, and there is also the absence of it. So, whenever we think about anything we desire – whether it's money, success, fun or fulfillment – we are focused either on its presence or on its absence. When we focus on the absence of what we want, we feel bad and we attract more lack. When we focus on the presence of what we want, we feel good and we magnetize to ourselves the things we desire.

Imagine holding a stick in your hands. On one end of the stick you have what you DON'T WANT, and on the other end you have what you DO WANT. It's you who chooses which end of the stick to focus on!

Understanding the Law of Polarity is the secret that lets you stop getting what you don't want and start getting more of what you do want.

When you're aware of the polarity of the Universe and start applying the Law of Polarity in your life, you're using your power to deliberately create what you want instead of feeling like you're a victim to life events and circumstances.

It is you who decides where to put your FOCUS when a challenge crosses your path. And whatever you choose to focus on, you will create more of!

When you know the Law of Polarity, you can choose how you want to respond to what is happening instead of just reacting. Your ability to choose your response is your greatest power.

You have learnt in this book that what you feel, you also attract. That nothing is more important than that you feel good. In any challenging situation, you can choose to focus on what you want – instead of what you don't want – and in doing so, raise your energetic frequency and feel better. And whenever you feel better, you will also draw better things and experiences to you. When you feel better, you're able to move towards what you want with much more ease.

Imagine how it would feel for you to be able to respond rather than react whenever a challenging situation arises. Instead of being stuck in doubt, you can choose to focus on hope. Instead of worry, you can choose to focus on peace. Instead of judging and beating yourself up, you can choose compassion and self-care. You have the choice, always. And whatever you choose will affect the results you manifest.

You cannot create a happy and fulfilling life filled with joy, passion and success with a mind focused on the unwanted and negative. Knowing the Law of Polarity gives you the opportunity to choose what you FOCUS on: what you don't want or what you do want. This is your power, and it's a power that nothing and nobody can take away from you!

I Am Moving from Lack to Abundance!

I was halfway through my one-year-long studies to become a life coach. I was truly happy and excited about my new path and all the amazing things waiting for me.

However, there was one big BUT: I was still without a job! Each month, I was going deeper into debt as I continued paying for my studies. My financial situation was increasingly worrying me. I needed to find a job. I needed consistent income.

Of course, I was doing all the things one is supposed to do when looking for a job. I was going through job announcements every week. I was filling out job applications. I was even invited to a few interviews – but even though the interviews went well, I didn't end up being the candidate they chose for the position. I felt stuck.

As I was learning about the Universal Laws and manifestation principles, I knew that I must be standing in my own way. I knew that the reason I had not yet gotten a job was in me. I knew that I was not in energetic alignment with the job I was looking for. Energetically, I was not a match to what I wanted! A part of me wanted to find a job, but there was also a part of me that was in resistance and did not feel good about it.

Yes, you read that right: a part of me did not want a job! All the potential jobs looked boring and draining. The whole process of filling out applications was just something I had to do; there was no excitement. I had a very hard time imagining that I could find a job I'd be satisfied with. I was also afraid that a day job would demand too much of my energy and would stand in the way of my dream career as a coach.

Can you manifest something into your life from a place of disbelief, doubt and not feeling good about it? Hardly. I knew I needed help to get out of my own way!

I asked an experienced coach, Debbie, who I'd heard great things about, to help me with my "big issue." As I was already seeing how many positive changes coaching can bring into people's lives, I hoped very much that coaching would help me too.

And here's what happened... After a single one-hour coaching session, I was feeling completely different about the job I was looking for. I was full of positive expectation. I was feeling good. I was seeing new options!

In the coaching session, Debbie helped me shift my focus from all the things I didn't feel good about – everything I DID NOT WANT in a job and everything that bothered me – to everything I DID WANT in a job.

After the coaching session, I was now looking for a job that I truly wanted! I was looking for a job:

- *with supportive and nice colleagues;*
- *that I found easy and enjoyed;*
- *that made me feel confident and successful;*
- *that had defined working hours so I could pursue my dream career as a coach (very important for me!); and*
- *that I was happy to wake up to.*

For the first time in a very long time, I felt hopeful and excited about the possibility of finding a job that I liked and that could be a great fit for me!

Are you curious to know the end of the story?

Just two weeks after the coaching session with Debbie, I started a job as a customer service representative at a governmental agency that was helping unemployed people. I couldn't believe it! I felt on top of the world!!

Not only did I manifest a job, but this job turned out to be the first job in my life(!) that I was truly happy and excited to wake up to every day! Can you believe it?

It was my first job where I was dealing with customers. I enjoyed so much being with so many people and helping them. I liked my colleagues.

I loved helping customers. I felt like I could totally be myself. I felt valued and appreciated.

I didn't have a fancy job title. My salary was lower than I was used to. But I was feeling truly happy. This job was exactly what I needed, as it aligned perfectly with my plans to become a coach and my future vision!

I was now pursuing my dream and I also had a day job – not only one that supported me financially, but also one that I liked very much!

The Power of Your Focus

Once you understand that the Law of Polarity is working all the time – that there are two poles of everything – you realize that every problem in your life is also an opportunity. Every challenge you face is also a chance. Every setback you experience is also a possibility.

When you start viewing your life from this perspective, you will feel empowered. You'll feel that you're in the driver's seat of your life instead of being a passive passenger in the back seat.

Now, let's be clear: This is not to say that your perspective will save you from feeling pain, disappointment or sorrow. That is not possible. These feelings will always be part of your life journey.

But when you start looking at your setbacks as opportunities, you will not let yourself stay stuck in the low energy feelings. You'll be able to rise up and continue your journey after each setback with renewed energy, hope and determination.

So often, we cannot see the opportunity because we're so accustomed to giving our full focus to the problem.

Let's take a closer look at one challenging situation you might be facing: feeling stuck in your current job. Your energy level is low. You feel exhausted. Your constant stress keeps you up at night.

You keep showing up and doing what needs to be done, because you have to. There is no joy or excitement. You've already submitted a few applications for other jobs, but this hasn't yielded any results yet. Deep inside, you're also worried about whether you'll be able to get a new job. Why should they choose you, you think, when there are so many qualified candidates? You feel stuck on a hamster wheel.

Let's look at how you can apply the Law of Polarity in this challenging situation to help you move forward.

You can keep focusing on your current job that is draining your energy, causing frustration and making you unhappy. You can keep thinking about how unfair life is, and that you surely deserve so much better. You can call your friends and family to share your frustration and worry and to complain about the situation. So many people jump into this complaining mode when faced with a challenging situation.

All these feelings and thoughts are totally normal and valid. It's okay to allow yourself to feel what you feel. It's okay to feel sadness, disappointment or discouragement.

But what you need to realize is that what you focus on, you will attract more of. The Law of Attraction will always give you more of the way you feel. The more you focus on what you DON'T WANT – the current job situation that is making you miserable – the more stuck and powerless you'll feel.

You've got to decide to SHIFT YOUR FOCUS to what you DO WANT. Period. Only then will you be able to raise your energy and start feeling better. As you start feeling better, you'll start attracting better things and experiences. You will no longer be stuck.

Every challenge is an opportunity to gain clarity about what you truly want. Instead of focusing on the current job that you don't want, you need to change your focus to what you do want. Here are some questions you can ask yourself to help you change your focus:

o   What type of job would make me truly happy?
o   What people would I love to work with?
o   What activities within a job would make me feel excited and energized?
o   What job would allow me to feel more alive and use my passions and gifts?

Here's the thing. The more you start focusing on what you DO WANT, the better you will start feeling in your present situation, and the faster you will start seeing positive shifts in your life.

You might be thinking, "But isn't that denying reality and pretending that the problems don't exist?"

I totally understand why you might think this way. But one thing is for sure: What you FOCUS on, you ATTRACT. If you don't want to stay where you are, you need to change your focus! Your reality cannot change if you don't change your focus.

Either you keep focusing on what you don't want and keep attracting more of the same, or you change your focus towards what you do want and move forward with ease.

Abraham Hicks says this powerfully: "You can't create a new reality while you've got your undivided attention upon the reality that exists." You've got to shift your focus!

Remember that nothing is more important than that you feel good. Only when you feel good do you become a match to new and better things and experiences.

Let's Put it into Action

Exercise

Instant Mood Booster

This exercise will help you get back to FEELING GOOD every time you face a challenging situation, problem or setback.

As soon as you're facing a situation that negatively affects your feeling state, get into the habit of asking yourself the following two questions:

- What do I WANT?

- How do I want to FEEL?

Example:

Your colleague or family member has said something hurtful and you just cannot let go of the comment. You're in a bad mood, and you keep thinking about what they said and how unfair it is.

Instead of letting yourself continue feeling sad, disappointed or discouraged, pause and ask yourself:

o   What do I WANT?

Your answer may be that you want to be respected, loved and accepted for who you are. You want to be with people who are kind and nice to you.

o   How do I want to FEEL?

Your answer may be that you want to feel calm, peaceful, relaxed and confident. As you're thinking about how you want to feel, try to connect to these feelings and feel them in your body.

These two questions will help you shift your focus and your feeling state immediately!

Remember, as you feel, so you attract. The better you feel, the more easily you will move forward and the better things and experiences you will attract.

Use these two questions whenever you run into challenges, big or small. Don't forget that it doesn't serve you to stay in low energy emotions – it is important that you shift yourself to feeling better!

CHAPTER 8

WANT IT AND
LET IT GO!

Y ou're probably like most ambitious people: You make a plan, you take action and you want to see results as you move along. You are results-oriented.

You can't wait to see the evidence that things are going according to your plan, that you're moving closer to your goal with each step you take. Right?

Being results-focused is great. Wanting to see progress as you move along is great!

But here's the thing... If you are so focused on things going according to your time schedule and in your own way, you become too attached to the outcome. And guess what happens when you're too attached to the outcome or the result that you want?

When you're too focused on the result, you're no longer present in the now. You are no longer open to the life that is unfolding right before you, in this very moment. You are no longer enjoying and feeling great in this very moment. You get impatient or maybe doubtful or worried when things don't seem to go exactly as you expected.

The truth is that being too attached to the outcome you're aiming at will often bring you further away from the very thing that you so deeply desire. When you are too attached, you are getting in your own way.

Get ready to discover the secret that so many ambitious, talented and hard-working individuals are not aware of when they set out to reach big goals. It's a secret that will help you stay the course no matter what is happening in your life and manifest what you want with ease and without hustle. It's the secret of LETTING GO…

The Law of Detachment

In order to manifest your deepest dreams and desires, you need to know and master the Law of Detachment.

This law works in harmony with all the other Universal Laws you're learning in this book to help you create the life you desire and manifest your dreams.

The Law of Detachment states that in order to acquire anything in the physical Universe, you must relinquish your attachment to it. Relinquishing attachment means that you are not attached to the thing you want to achieve, or that you are detached from it.

What does it mean "not to be attached" to the thing you want?

People often have a hard time believing that they're going to reach their goals and desires. They get impatient and frustrated when they don't see results right away, or when things don't go as expected. They get easily discouraged when they don't see evidence that they are succeeding, or when they lack approval from others. All such feelings mean that they are "attached" to the outcome that they want.

When you are attached to the result, you lack trust. The Law of Detachment is all about TRUST. You move forward trusting and knowing that things will unfold in a perfect way and will come to you in their own perfect time. There is no need to worry, doubt or feel impatient.

To be detached from the outcome also means reaching for your goals and desires while simultaneously staying present in the now. Be present and open to all the ways your life is unfolding right in front of you.

Of course you need to take action. Of course you need to want whatever you want with all your heart. But you need to TRUST in the process of life. You need to have faith that all is going to be well. You need to believe that the Universe is always on your side, and that your dreams and desires will come to you in their own best time.

When you know the Law of Detachment and apply it to creating what you want in your life, you will experience great peace and relief. You will feel good in the now – which is exactly how you need to feel in order to manifest whatever you want.

When you feel good in the now, you are in alignment with your desires and you are open to receiving them! You are enjoying the journey.

When you feel good in the now, you are detached from the outcome and you are going with the flow. The flow of life is going to take you wherever you want to go, with ease and without struggle.

Staying detached from the outcome also means being open to the magic of life and its unexpected surprises. When you're fully enjoying the journey, you are open to receiving something even better than you could imagine!

Let Go of Your Time Schedule

So many people stand in their own way because they have a strong need for things to unfold according to their plan, and they have too many expectations about how they should be moving forward.

As soon as they encounter obstacles or setbacks, they begin to hold themselves back. They start doubting whether they are good enough. They start hesitating, getting impatient or discouraged. They start worrying about what others will think. They might even start thinking that the path they've chosen may be not for them, because things should unfold much easier.

Can you perhaps relate?

All such feelings that arise when things are not going according to your plan are an indication that you are not in harmony with the Law of Detachment, which is all about trusting and knowing that things are unfolding as they should.

You need to believe in your dream, move towards it, and at the same time be detached from your ideas of HOW and WHEN things will come to you. Release your need for things to manifest based on your time schedule and in the way you think they should appear in your life!

You need to want the things that you desire, but you also need to LET GO. Joe Vitale says it so beautifully: "When you state your intention and let it go, you give your unconscious mind and the Universe a chance to begin working on bringing it to you."

The more you let go of your expectations about WHEN and HOW things are going to happen, the more you'll enjoy your journey. The more you let go of your need for things to happen on your timeline, the better you'll feel and the more open you'll be to receiving what you want.

Your desires are meant to become your reality! The Universe is always on your side, but you need to move out of your own way... Whenever you're feeling doubtful, hesitant, discouraged or impatient, you are blocking your desire from coming into your life.

To receive what you want, you must allow your desire to come to you. To allow is to feel good in the now. To be unattached to what you want. The happier you feel in your now, the more you allow your desire to manifest.

Remember that the energy you send out comes back to you. What you feel is what you attract. Nothing is more important than that you feel good!

When you are feeling low energy emotions, such as fear, worry or doubt, you are attracting the same energy to you. Nothing good can be created when you're feeling bad. Only when you feel good can you expect good things and experiences to come into your life.

Feeling good is allowing yourself to receive what you want. Feeling good is being unattached to when and how things will come to you. Feeling good is going with the flow and allowing your desires to come to you in their own best time!

I Manifested My First Client!

I still couldn't believe that Jack had agreed to work with me as a coaching client.

"I've got my first paying client!! Thank you, Universe!" I remember wanting to shout out loud and jump for joy.

Jack was the first client to join the three-month coaching program I'd created after I became a certified coach. I felt on top of the world! I truly felt he was a perfect match for my program. Our conversation on the first call was filled with ease. It was smooth. He even wanted to pay in full for the whole program right away, even though I also offered a payment plan option.

And you know what was so amazing about this experience? I manifested my first paying client when I least expected it. Really! He came out of the blue.

Now let me explain. Of course I planned to attract paying clients for my program, as I was investing time and energy into creating it. But here's the thing: I was not attached to the outcome. I was not attached to WHEN or HOW people would join my program. I was not in need. I was just doing the work and truly enjoying it.

When Jack booked a call with me to discover more about the program, I showed up to the call being totally okay with the result, whether he wanted to join my program or not. Would it be nice if he joined? Yes. But I did not expect a specific outcome. I showed up with the best intention and without expectation.

My experience with getting my first client is a perfect example of what it looks like when you are not attached to the outcome. I was clear about what I wanted: I knew what type of people I wanted to help. I did the work by creating the program and sharing it on my social media and in my network. And I did not have any need for a client to show up at a certain time or in a certain way. I wanted it and let it go. I was feeling good.

When you do the work and let it go, when you're detached from the outcome, that is when you allow for the things you want to manifest!

I still sometimes have to remind myself of how important it is to want something and let it go. It's easy to forget this when you're working on something important and things just don't seem to go as planned. Luckily, I know what I have to do in such situations!

As soon as I start feeling impatient, worried or doubtful, I pause and remind myself that my job is to focus on what I want, take action and let go of all expectations regarding HOW and WHEN things come to me. My job is to feel good as I move along, because only when I feel good am I in alignment with what I want!

Today, when I see my clients getting upset or disappointed that things aren't going the way they expected, the very first piece of advice I give them is to do anything they can to make themselves feel better. You see, it's all about the energy you put out. You cannot manifest things you want from a place of neediness or discouragement, no matter how hard you push. You need to feel good! You need to be detached from the outcome.

Trusting the Universe

Your ego wants to be in control. The ego needs things to go according to plan and loves evidence of success and approval from others. It loves to predict outcomes and will feel unsafe with every change.

For the ego, every setback is a threat and every "no" feels like a defeat. This is exactly why so many lose the momentum towards achieving their desires and dreams as soon as they experience a challenge or disappointment.

The truth is that your journey – especially when you dare go after your deepest desires and dreams – will seldom go as planned. There will be obstacles. There will be unexpected events and challenges.

If you keep viewing everything that happens to you only from the logical perspective, you'll often feel that things are not going as they should. You will be easily disappointed and discouraged. You may start doubting yourself, hesitating or procrastinating. You might conclude that you're just not good enough or not smart enough. You might even decide that you're not meant to succeed.

Here's the thing. If you only listen to your mind and let your ego guide you, you will almost never reach your destination.

The path to your greatest success is the path where you must be guided by your heart. Of course you've got to take your mind with you – but you must let your heart lead the way! You must follow your inner guidance, which is guidance from the Universe that wants the best for you and that will guide you through every challenge that comes your way.

You must move forward TRUSTING the Universe.

What if the unexpected challenge that you're facing is exactly what you need right now in order to be able to reach your destination? The Universe would never have given you the challenge in the first place if it was not for your higher good. Maybe the challenge that you're facing is going to teach you a lesson without which you won't be able to succeed in the next step.

From the ego's point of view, it appears that you are the one controlling the manifestation of your desires. That you know the best way. But you don't. Your mind does not see the bigger picture of your life. It sees only a tiny fraction of the bigger picture.

The Universe has a big picture of your life. It knows the most direct pathway to your desires and dreams. And it leads you to your destination through your inner guidance.

Your job is to focus on the end result you're reaching for, take action and TRUST that whatever is happening in your life is happening for your higher good and will take you exactly where you want to be. In its own perfect time.

And guess what happens when you move forward enjoying the journey and feeling good along the way? You know the answer, don't you? The Law of Attraction will give you even more things to enjoy!

Treat each challenging experience as part of the Universe's plan to get you where you want to be. Trust the Universe.

Let's Put it into Action

Exercise

Act As If You Have It

This exercise will raise your energetic vibration and help you let go of any resistance you might have regarding manifesting your goals and desires. The less you worry about how you're going to get what you want, the more open you are to receiving it!

1. Pick a goal or desire that you want to bring into your life. It can be big or small.

   Maybe it's a new job, more money, a new and more fulfilling relationship, a healthy and fit body, a dream vacation, writing a book... It can be anything you truly want!

2. Go ahead and imagine that you've already reached your goal or desire. How is your life when you have what you want? Let your imagination run free and act as if you have it!

3. Tune into your feelings: How are you FEELING when you have it already? Is it joy, success, excitement, appreciation, love? FEEL these emotions now.

Do this exercise as often as you'd like to!

Acting as if you already have what you want and feeling the emotions is a powerful, easy and fun way to speed up the manifestation!

Remember, the better you feel, the faster and more easily you move towards anything you want!

CHAPTER 9

SELF-LOVE

⸺⸻◈⸻⸺

As you're going through the pages of this book, you're learning about the Laws of the Universe and how to apply them in your life so that you can create what you desire and manifest your dreams.

Knowing the Universal Laws is like knowing the rules of the game. Yet even if you do your best to play by the rules, you still won't be able to achieve true happiness and fulfillment if you miss one fundamental thing: self-love. You've got to LOVE yourself!

The more you love yourself, the more easily you'll move towards all you want, and the more joy, success and fulfillment you will experience. No challenge or setback is too big when you love YOU.

Your outer world is the direct reflection of your inner world. The more you value and love yourself, the more love you will see and experience in the outer world.

Your journey towards your most amazing life starts with self-love. And actually, you already have proof that you love yourself: you've decided that you want more out of life and you no longer want to stay where you are. That's self-love!

Self-love is the foundation for your success, happiness and wellbeing. It is the fuel that you need on your journey towards creating your most amazing life. Without the fuel, you won't be able to reach your destination.

Only when you truly love yourself will you be able to be, do and have all you want!

Accepting Yourself as You Are

Most people have learnt to appreciate and feel good about themselves when they succeed at something, or when they get something they wanted. So much of their happiness and self-worth depends on their accomplishments and their performance.

Likewise, many of us are taught to appreciate and feel good about ourselves when others give us validation and approval. The more praise and acknowledgement we get from others, the better we feel about ourselves.

There is nothing wrong with feeling good about yourself when you succeed at something or when you get praise from others. However, feeling happy about yourself when things are going well for you and when others show you appreciation is only a small part of what self-love is.

TRUE SELF-LOVE is feeling and knowing your value irrespective of your achievements and how others view you. True self-love is not based on any conditions. It is loving yourself exactly as you are, in this very moment. Loving yourself just the way you are. With all you've accomplished and haven't accomplished yet. With all you're good at and all you struggle with. Loving yourself when others approve of you and when they criticize you.

True self-love is loving yourself unconditionally. It's feeling that you are enough exactly as you are.

"But if I just accept and approve of myself exactly as I am, doesn't that mean I won't feel the need to strive, to become better and work hard to reach my goals?" you may think.

No! Of course you need to take action and do your best in order to create the life you desire and manifest your dreams!

SELF-LOVE means that you commit to accepting and loving yourself all throughout your journey, no matter what happens. It means you stay loving and kind to yourself when there are ups and downs. When things are going your way and doors open easily, and when setbacks cross your way. When you try and succeed, and when you try and fail. When others applaud you and when others judge you.

Self-love means that you do not allow your successes or your failures to define who you are and your worth. It means you keep being strong, confident and connected to your value no matter what happens. You have faith that all is going to be well. You do not let your outer life circumstances or other people determine how you feel about yourself.

When you truly LOVE YOURSELF, you are not afraid to fail, because failure does not define who you are. Failure is just a part of your journey that makes you wiser, stronger and more resilient.

When you truly love yourself, the ups and downs on your path do not shake you. They do not affect the essence of who you are. Because who you are is enough, no matter what happens.

When you are filled with self-love, you choose to have faith that all will be well and to keep going no matter what.

Self-love is knowing and feeling your value, which does not depend on outer circumstances and conditions, skills or accomplishments. Your inner value.

The more you LOVE YOURSELF, the more love you will experience from the world. Love attracts love. The more you love yourself, the more love you will be able to give. When you truly love yourself, you naturally become loving to the people you meet on your way! When you see your value, you will see their value, and they will feel it.

When you love yourself unconditionally, everything becomes possible! As Louise Hay said so beautifully, "Love is the great miracle cure. Loving ourselves works miracles in our lives."

Making Self-Care Your Priority

As you've learnt already in this book, nothing is more important than that you feel good. The energy that you are sending out comes back to you. To be able to move towards fulfillment of your goals and dreams, you must be feeling good on a daily basis!

Commitment to taking care of yourself and how you feel is an act of self-love.

Decide that feeling good and your wellbeing matter to you and that from now on, you will make self-care your top priority!

Let's face it: Everything in your daily life affects the way you feel. Everything! Your job. Your daily habits. The food you eat. The thoughts you engage in. The people you surround yourself with. The movies you watch. The books you read.

Take a closer look at your life and start asking yourself what changes you need to make so that you can take better care of yourself and feel better.

Maybe there are habits that are draining your energy? Not enough sleep, lack of exercise, too much time on the couch in front of the TV? Maybe you're lacking excitement and joy as you're going through the motions, day in and day out, because you don't have any time left for yourself and things that speak to your heart?

Decide that your energy matters! Start exercising regularly, get enough sleep, choose healthier food! Meditate a few minutes a day. Ask yourself what brings you joy and commit to spending some time every week on activities that lift your mood and raise your energy. All these small changes will raise your vibration and help you move towards your goals and desires with much more ease. Never forget that as you feel, so you attract!

Maybe you often end up saying YES to things that, deep inside, you don't want? Maybe there are people in your life, even friends, who do not try to understand you or support you, or who even try to belittle you, hurt you or make you feel less-than?

Decide to check in with yourself first before saying YES to anything or anyone. Every time you say YES to something that, deep inside, you want to say NO to, you're not being true to yourself and your inner voice.

Decide that your mental and emotional wellbeing matters and distance yourself from people who do not respect or appreciate you. If you cannot distance yourself, try to set a boundary or limit the amount of time you spend with them. Standing up for yourself and setting boundaries is an act of self-love! Setting boundaries means that you honor yourself and take responsibility for the way you feel and the energy you allow into your life.

You deserve to be with people who see the best in you, love you for who you are and want you to win! When you are in the company of people who are rooting for you and your success, you will be inspired and motivated to move forward and go after your dreams.

Taking care of yourself, how you feel and what energy you allow into your life is self-love. Loving yourself is all about making daily choices that help you feel good and honor who you are and that are aligned with your goals and desires!

Falling in Love with Me

Studying to become a coach was also a journey of a deep personal transformation for me. Not only was I becoming a life coach – I was also becoming a new person who loved myself more and more and who was now committed to my passions and dreams!

Never before had I been so in tune with my inner guidance.

Previously, I would second-guess myself and overthink things before making a decision; now, I was much more clear about whether or not I wanted to do something. I just followed my inner guidance.

Previously, I would dismiss any unkind remark and pretend that it didn't affect me; now, I allowed myself to fully acknowledge how I was feeling. I started speaking up and setting boundaries. I no longer allowed people into my life who were not loving and kind and who didn't care about my feelings. I was committed to loving and valuing me!

Previously, I would easily say YES to things even if, deep inside, I did not want to do them; now, I was being honest with myself and checking in with my feelings to see if this was really something I wanted to do. I was now no longer afraid to say NO. The more I started to value myself, my time and my energy, the more ready and willing I was to say NO without feeling guilty. I was now only willing to say YES to things that served me or that contributed positively to my life. My time and energy are valuable!

The more I valued and accepted myself, the more clear it became that I only needed to be surrounded with friends who truly valued me for who I was and who wanted the best for me. Friends who loved me unconditionally. Friends who supported me on my new path and who were able to understand me. I wanted to be with people with whom I could be fully myself.

I realized that some friendships needed to end, and I now had the courage to walk away. I could no longer afford to have people in my close circle who did not see me for who I was, or did not want the best for me. In fact, I had realized long before starting my journey as a coach that some of my friendships were no longer good for me and no longer added value to my life. But it was only now that I had gained the courage to decide it was time to move on. I deserved to be with people with whom I could share excitement and joy in my new journey and whom I truly wanted to have in my life!

After so many years of doing my best to be a nice person who cared so much about other people's feelings, I was now becoming a person who was committed to being nice to myself. I started to stand up for myself when needed. I was now a person who valued, appreciated and loved me for who I was. It felt great.

I felt so blessed that I was not alone on my new journey. I was part of a supportive and loving community at the Quantum Success Coaching Academy, which became like my new family. I was with so many others who were committed to their growth, expansion and an intention to live the best life possible.

Treating Yourself with Compassion

Another aspect of self-love is treating yourself with kindness and compassion. Always. No matter what. Compassion is a game-changer!

So many of us are used to judging and criticizing ourselves and others when things are not going as expected or when we experience setbacks or failure. Likewise, so many of us look back at our life with regret that things did not go as we wanted them to, or that we didn't know better.

Self-judgement, guilt and regret are low energy emotions that will only keep you unhappy. Yes! Because like energy draws like energy.

Whenever you find yourself feeling guilt, regret or disappointment, embrace yourself in compassion. Let the energy of COMPASSION fill your mind and body. Compassion will help you transform any negative emotions and make you instantly feel better. Whenever you feel better, you attract better, and you're in a position to choose thoughts that are more positive and uplifting!

The more you let go and forgive yourself for everything that's happened in the past, and the more you release the lower energy from your mind and body, the more you raise your vibration. The higher your vibration, the more magnetic you are to all the good things that the Universe wants to offer you!

The same is true for all the people who hurt you in the past. Maybe you still feel the hurt in your heart and body. Decide to let go and forgive them!

So many people think that holding on to the resentment and not forgiving the other person is the right thing to do, because the person does not deserve to be "let off the hook." These feelings are normal and valid; allow yourself to feel them.

But you have to understand that when you hold on to resentment and don't forgive, you are first and foremost hurting yourself. You are allowing the lower energies of resentment and hurt to reside in your body, which affects your entire energy system and what you attract. Your feelings of resentment or hate do not affect the person they are directed towards – your feelings affect YOU.

If you still have people in your life who you have a hard time forgiving, be honest about how you feel and embrace yourself in compassion. Be kind and gentle to yourself. Compassion will bring you back to calm, peace and wellbeing and will help you release any hard and unpleasant feelings.

Choose to FORGIVE. Forgiveness is self-love. There is so much relief and power in forgiveness. Forgiveness will make you free and will allow you to get unstuck and move towards all you want with ease.

Forgiveness is for YOU. Not for them. Choose to forgive because you deserve to have all your dreams and desires come true!

Love and compassion for yourself is the key to your peace, happiness and all that you want!

Let's Put it into Action

Exercise

Open Yourself to Love

1. Sit comfortably in a quiet place and start by gently closing your eyes. Take a few deep breaths, being aware of the breath as it enters and leaves your body. Let go of any thoughts or concerns and allow yourself to relax and settle fully into this moment.

2. Imagine that at the top of your head there is a beautiful golden ball of light. See the light flowing down through the top of your head into your mind, your throat and down to your chest, lighting up your heart. Feel the warmth and expansion in your heart. Continue to see the light going down through your arms, your spine, your belly, your hips and all the way down your legs and your feet. See your entire body filled with and surrounded by the bright golden light.

3. Allow this golden light to clear any energy from your body that you do not want, and feel completely relaxed and in total wellbeing and peace. Sit for a few minutes in this state of calm, bliss and serenity. If any thoughts arise, just let them come and go and turn your attention back to your breath.

4. As you are sitting in this peaceful state and your body is filled with and surrounded by light, say these words to yourself silently:

    o   I am loved and supported
    o   All is well in my world

o   I live in a loving Universe

o   I am precious and lovable

Repeat these words a few times. As you say them, tune into the truth of these words and feel the love and support from the Universe. (You can choose to say any other words that you want and that feel good to you too!)

5. When you feel ready, slowly start drawing your attention to your breath and open your eyes. Have the intention to carry this experience with you as you return to your daily activities.

You can do this practice in the morning, evening or any other time of day that suits you to remind yourself that you are always loved, cared for and supported.

CHAPTER 10

ALL IS POSSIBLE

••⸱⸱⸱⸱⸱⸱⸱⸱⸱⸱⸱⸱⸱⸱⸱⸱⸱⸱⸱⸱⸱⸱·◈«◇»◈·⸱⸱⸱⸱⸱⸱⸱⸱⸱⸱⸱⸱⸱⸱⸱⸱⸱⸱⸱⸱⸱⸱••

Time to celebrate! You have reached the last chapter of the book! Aren't you feeling excited to be on this transformational journey that will lead you to your dreams and desires? Isn't it deeply fulfilling to know that you can be, do and have everything that you want – as long as you keep moving forward, have faith and do your best to feel good?

If you desire something, you can have it. If you dream about something, you can have it. No doubt about that! You are the creator of your future and you can manifest all that you want.

You live in a Universe that is filled with infinite possibilities. There are no limits in the Universe for what you can create. Nothing is impossible. Only your mind sets limits for what you can have and achieve.

Get ready to discover how you can tune into the infinite possibilities of the Universe so that you have unshakable belief in yourself and your vision and become unstoppable in the pursuit of your dreams, happiness and fulfillment.

Your amazing future is waiting for you!

The Law of Pure Potentiality

The Law of Pure Potentiality is the last Universal Law that you need to understand and apply in your life in order to create what you want and manifest your dreams.

This law is based on the fact that the source of all creation is pure consciousness or pure potentiality seeking to express itself into form.

Another way of saying it is that everything is ENERGY. All energy wants to move, to create, to play, to expand. Energy is always seeking expression into some type of form.

As you hold a vision of what you want to create, energy seeks expression into what you want to create. Yes, energy is constantly taking on form according to your needs and desires. Where your focus goes, energy flows!

When you realize that you live in a Universe that is full of INFINITE POSSIBILITIES, you are then in alignment with the power that manifests everything in the Universe. Anything is possible, and there is unlimited creativity. The only limits are the ones you have in your mind.

How do you feel when you sit and watch a sunset? Or when you look at the stars on a summer night? Or when you listen to the waves of the ocean crash up against the shore? Pure potentiality created all this...

The desires and dreams that you have inside you come from pure potentiality. Not from your mind. They come from the infinite field of possibilities.

When you align yourself with the Law of Pure Potentiality, you feel free, fearless and powerful. You know that you can create all you want in your life. Nothing is impossible.

When you are connected to the field of pure potentiality, you know that there is potential for all of it. You are in alignment with the true nature of who you are. You are open to receive all that you want!

When you look at your goals and dreams from the perspective of your mind, you will always find limitations to how far you can go. But when you allow yourself to tune into your imagination and the infinite potential of the Universe, you will know that ALL IS POSSIBLE.

There is potential for you to live your passion and purpose and make the impact you desire to make. There is potential for you to be full of health and vitality. There is potential for you to find true love, manifest abundance, create outrageous success and all you dream of.

Because there is potential in the infinite field of possibilities for all the things that you desire to have, you can have it all. You are the deliberate creator of your life and you can have all you want!

Holding the Future Vision

The key to manifesting your future goals, desires and dreams is to constantly keep your focus on your Future Vision.

As you HOLD THE VISION of what you desire in front of you and never lose sight of it, over time, it has to manifest!

The more you focus on your Future Self who is living the life that you dream of, and the more you tune into the energy of your Future Self, the faster and more easily you'll find yourself moving towards all that you want. Your focus is your power.

The core principle of quantum physics states that our past, present and future exist at the same time. The future version of you living your dream life exists already in the quantum field. And because it already exists in the quantum field, it has the potential to become your reality. How amazing is that?!

As you always have connection to your past, so you can connect to your future in your present. Your past experiences and memories affect your present reality. In the same way, your present life is affected by the vision and expectations you have for your future.

The more you, in your current reality, allow yourself to dwell on the past and everything that didn't go the way you wanted, the slower your progress towards your dreams and desires will be. On the contrary, the more you, in your current reality, FOCUS ON YOUR

FUTURE SELF and all the amazing things waiting for you, the faster you'll move towards all you want!

Your thoughts and feelings in the present moment affect your future! As the deliberate creator of your life, you have to actively choose where you want to put your focus. The more you focus on your Future Vision, and the more your energetic frequency matches the energy of your desires and dreams, the faster you will manifest what you want! You must be in alignment with the energy that you want to bring in!

Your job is to HOLD FOCUS ON YOUR VISION as much as possible. The less attention you give to the present reality and all its problems and limitations, the faster you will move towards the future you desire. The more attention you give to the Future Vision, and the more excited, happy and passionate you feel, the more easily you will manifest all that you want into your life.

You don't need to wait to feel joy. You can tap into freedom, joy, success, love and fulfillment now. All these feelings exist in the field of pure potentiality and you can tap into them now!

As Bob Proctor said, "You are already connected to everything you desire. If you want to attract it, you must be on the same frequency."

Everything is energy, and energy creates. The more you imagine yourself living your dream life already, the more you will draw back to you things, situations and experiences that will help you get what you want. How amazing is that?

Meditation

When you are connected to the field of infinite possibilities, you feel peace, calm and clarity.

One of the key ways to tune into the field of infinite potentiality is through meditation.

Have you ever tried to meditate? If so, you've most likely already experienced the positive effects it can bring to your state of being.

The benefits of MEDITATION are incredible. It brings peace and calm. It makes you feel grounded. It brings you clarity and makes you feel powerful. It helps you let go of any stress, overwhelm or low energy feelings such as sadness, discouragement or disappointment. If you choose to meditate consistently, it will change your life in so many positive ways!

It is in the stillness of your mind that your best ideas come to you and solutions to your problems arise.

When it comes to creating your dream life, nothing is more important than that you feel good. Meditation will always raise your energy and make you feel better! Moreover, when you meditate, you let go of any resistance you might feel about creating what you want. Resistance comes from your mind and your limiting thoughts and beliefs.

Only when your MIND IS QUIET can you vividly see yourself living your dreams and desires. Only when you are calm and at peace can you be free from any doubts, hesitation or disbelief. Through meditation, you can allow yourself to fully tune into the field of pure potentiality where your Future Self has already achieved all that you want and is living with joy, success and purpose.

The more you, in your present reality, can envision and feel that you're already living your dream life, the more you are drawing the dreams and desires to you.

Meditation also allows you to connect to your INNER GUIDANCE. The more in tune you are with your inner guidance, the more easily and effortlessly you will move towards all that you want. Your inner guidance comes from pure potentiality and is here to lead you on your journey to what you want in the best and easiest way for YOU.

Your mind might not know all the steps you need to take to make your dream your reality. But your inner guidance does! It knows exactly how to take you from wherever you are today to the fulfillment of your dreams. It will always guide you towards what is for your highest good and what will bring you joy. Follow your inner guidance and you will always be on the right path! How amazing is that? All you need to do is to tune into the field of pure potentiality through meditation and allow the inner guidance to speak to you.

There are so many ways you can meditate. Find your favorite way and make it into a daily habit. My absolute favorite way to meditate is to listen to guided meditations.

Too many people worry about whether they're meditating "the right way" as they try to focus on all the instructions for doing it "correctly"… Don't get hung up on all the instructions and technicalities! You don't have to be in a lotus position to meditate. Do it in whatever way feels right for you. Just a few minutes spent in silence with your eyes closed while being aware of your breath is perfect. Or taking a walk in nature as you listen to birds singing and the wind rustling the leaves on the trees. Or just lying down, relaxed and daydreaming.

If your meditation makes you feel good and you feel calm, refreshed and energized, you are doing it right. Remember that nothing is more important than that you feel good!

Meeting My Future Self

One of the most inspiring and mind-blowing discoveries that I had during my coaching studies was connecting to my Future Self.

Finding out that my Future Self – the Future Self that is living the life of my dreams and desires – already exists has been life-changing.

I remember clearly the first time I connected to my Future Self in a meditation. It was during one of the first classes at the academy. The experience was so beautiful, breathtaking and touching. I saw myself as a successful coach living the best life I could imagine – a life filled with passion, purpose, joy, love, success and abundance.

What I learnt was that the fastest and easiest way to create the amazing future I wanted was to connect to my Future Self in the present. This discovery was a game-changer!

Since I discovered this truth, my Future Self has become the guiding star in my daily life.

Whenever I'm feeling doubtful or disappointed because things aren't going my way, I get quiet and reconnect with my Future Self. This makes me immediately feel hopeful and grounded again. I find comfort and peace.

Whenever I get worried about the future, or even fearful about taking the next step or trying something new, I connect to my Future Self, which makes me immediately feel reassured, confident and uplifted.

Whenever I sense a feeling of boredom or lack of inspiration, I connect to my Future Self and I get my zest for life and my passion back.

My Future Self reminds me of where I'm going and of my WHY. It reminds me that all is possible if I just keep going and keep believing in myself and in my dreams.

When I connect to my Future Self, I know that all will be well and I am guided towards my next step.

I just lie down, get quiet, close my eyes and visualize different images and scenes from my Future Self's life. I feel the joy, success, love and fulfillment that my Future Self is living. It feels very real.

When I know that my future is bright, I feel empowered and inspired in my present. It gives me strength, peace and courage.

I don't want to let my past or my present determine what future I am going to live. I don't want to wait and see what the future has in store for me. I am the creator of my future! My Future Self that is living my most amazing life – the life of my dreams – already exists!

I know that nothing is more important than that I feel good in the now. My feelings are energy. When I feel good, I am projecting into the future that I want. When I am not feeling good, I am projecting into the future that I do not want.

The better I feel in the now, the faster and more easily I move towards my Future Self. The better I feel in the now, the more magnetic I am to all the good things and experiences that life has to offer.

All is well. I am on the right path. I am exactly where I need to be, and everything is unfolding in perfect order.

I am loved. I am guided. I move with ease.

My Future Self is waiting for me!

Stepping Into Your Future

1. Find a quiet place where you can be with yourself in peace for 15 to 20 minutes.

2. Sit or lie down and allow your body to find a position of comfort and ease. Gently close your eyes and take a few deep, slow breaths.

3. Picture in your mind your FUTURE SELF who is living the life of your dreams – the best life you can imagine! A life where all your desires and dreams have come true and you live with joy, success, abundance and purpose. Let yourself receive the images from your Future Self's life and enjoy the process fully.

4. Choose one scene from your Future Self's life – it can be anything! Go with your intuition. Maybe you're on your dream vacation, looking healthy, happy and energized. Maybe you're having a romantic dinner with the love of your life at your favorite restaurant on the beach. Maybe you're on stage, talking to hundreds of people about a project you're passionate about... Pick one scene that feels good!

5. Allow yourself to fully visualize as many details as you can in the chosen scene:

   o Where are you?
   o What time of day is it?

o What's the weather like?

o What do your surroundings look like?

o Who are you with?

o What do you look like?

o What are you doing?

o What are you saying?

6. Let yourself fully live into the experience as if it is happening NOW. How are you FEELING? Feel the joy, success, gratitude, peace, abundance, adventure… Feel these feelings NOW. Enjoy the sensations fully.

7. When you feel your experience is complete, turn your attention back to your breath and slowly return to the room where you're sitting or lying down. Before continuing your day, allow yourself to stay for a few moments with the feelings and sensations from this experience.

Connect to your Future Self as often as you want. The more you tune into the future version of you that is already living the life of your dreams, the faster you will be able to manifest all that you want!

YOUR AMAZING FUTURE IS WAITING FOR YOU!

Congratulations on reaching the end of this book! You did it. I am so proud of you!

What a journey it has been. I'd love to invite you to pause for a while and think about the person you were when you started reading this book and the person you are today. Can you see and feel the difference? I bet you can!

This book has taken you on a transformational journey of new discoveries, insights and learning. It is a journey of inner and outer changes leading you to live your best life – one that makes you happy, excited and fulfilled!

A transformational journey is never a straight line, nor is it an overnight experience. Like all great things, creating a life you love takes time. When we plant seeds, they do not sprout the next day – they sprout in their own time.

Here's what I want you to know before we conclude: Wherever you are on your journey today, it is perfectly fine. Know that you are exactly where you need to be, no matter how far you've come.

Maybe you have experienced big results already and manifested amazing things as you were going through this book. Or perhaps you think that you've been moving forward way too slowly, and you don't yet see any visible changes in your life. Or maybe you started your new journey with big plans and intentions, but life has gotten in your way.

Here's the truth. It's all good! Wherever you are today, it is perfectly fine. We are all unique. We are all on our unique journey. We all move forward in our own way. Know that you are exactly where you need to be and that things are unfolding exactly as they should.

Be patient. Be kind to yourself. Rest and recharge whenever you need. Embrace yourself with love and compassion when things are not going your way. Trust the process. Let go of the need for things to manifest on your plan and your time schedule, and trust that everything will come to you in its own time.

Focus on your vision daily. Believe in yourself. Keep taking those small steps every day towards your dreams, no matter what. Don't be hard on yourself. Take it easy and have more fun. You don't need to do things perfectly; you just need to get them done. Keep going!

This book has introduced you to the Universal Laws and how to use them in your life, which is the key to manifesting all that you want with ease and joy, and without hustle. You now have the knowledge and the tools to create a life you love and manifest your desires and dreams.

You are welcome to come back to this book again and again. You can read it from beginning to end, or you can simply listen to your intuition and dive into a chapter or exercise that speaks to you in the moment. Trust yourself and your inner guidance. You can't go wrong. The more you practice all that you have learnt in this book, the more masterful you will become as the creator of your life!

My heart is filled with joy and excitement as I think about YOU, the journey this book has taken you on and all the amazing things awaiting you!

Let the journey continue! I believe in you. I know you can be, do and have whatever you want. I know you can make it happen. I know there is greatness inside of you. You are unique, powerful and precious. Never, ever let doubt or disappointment get in the way of you moving towards your dreams!

My heart is full of gratitude to YOU because by reading this book, you have allowed me to be part of your amazing life experience.

If you would like to share your thoughts about this book or the experiences that this book has led you to have, or if you have any questions, you are always welcome to send me an email at info@daivaplath.com. I would love to hear from you!

If you want more support in applying the manifestation principles shared in this book to your life, or if you would like help in reaching your goals, desires and dreams, I invite you to schedule a Free Discovery Call with me, where I can share more of how I can work with you. You can book your Free Discovery Call and find more resources and information about personal coaching with me at www.daivaplath.com.

Keep going. What you want is on its way!

Much love,

Daiva

ACKNOWLEDGEMENTS

My heartfelt thanks go to Christy Whitman and the Quantum Success Coaching Academy, whose teachings have impacted my life in such a profound way. Becoming a certified Law of Attraction coach has set me on the path to following my passion and finding true joy and fulfilment in my life.

I am forever grateful to all those who have been and continue to be a great source of inspiration in my life journey: Abraham Hicks, Bob Proctor, Louise Hay, Eckhart Tolle, Joy Vitale, Rhonda Byrne, Janet Attwood, Nathalie Ledwell, Mary Morrissey, Wayne Dyer, Oliver Niño, Mandy Morris, Jeanna Gabellini, Christian Michelsen and many others.

A special thank you to Isse (Ismet Muratspahic) for inspiring me to write this book; his encouragement made the whole book-writing process so much easier than I thought it would be.

Thank you to xee_designs1 for a beautiful book cover and interior design.

My deepest thanks go to my darling Stefan for his love and always being by my side; to my mom and dad for their unconditional love, for always wanting the best for me and giving me the gift to dream and believe in myself; and to my brother for being the best brother I could wish for.

My heartfelt thanks go to my dear friends – I feel so grateful to share my life journey with you.

Thank you to my followers on LinkedIn for their support and encouragement, and to all those who've told me that my work has inspired them – it means the world to me!

My heart is full of gratitude to all my clients – to be a part of your life journey has been a privilege and a gift! I admire you for your willingness and commitment to reach for more and live your best life. Thank you for letting me do what I love most.

Finally, thank you, Universe, for all the amazing things in my life and for sending me the inspiration to write this book. I enjoyed every moment of it.

ABOUT THE AUTHOR

Daiva Plath is a transformational life coach helping ambitious individuals to reclaim their joy, power and passion and create a life of happiness, success and fulfillment.

For many years, Daiva longed to find joy and purpose in her life. Her search for truth and happiness led her into the world of personal development and coaching. In her forties, she discovered the Universal Laws and became a certified Law of Attraction coach, which was a turning point in her career and life.

Becoming a life coach has set Daiva on the path to finding joy, passion and fulfillment and creating a life she truly loves. Today, Daiva shares her knowledge, wisdom and passion with all those who are seeking to manifest their dreams and live with happiness, success and purpose. She has never been happier!

Before becoming a life coach, Daiva worked in the fields of public administration, project management, fund administration and customer service.

Daiva currently lives in Malmö, Sweden with her husband Stefan. She is originally from Lithuania but has lived most of her life in Denmark and Sweden. Apart from coaching and personal development, Daiva has a great passion for traveling and exploring new places.

For more information, resources and personal coaching, please visit www.daivaplath.com.

www.ingramcontent.com/pod-product-compliance
Lightning Source LLC
Chambersburg PA
CBHW022117280326
41933CB00007B/421